The Rhetoric of
Filmic Narration

Studies in Cinema, No. 12

Diane M. Kirkpatrick, Series Editor

Associate Professor, History of Art
The University of Michigan

Other Titles in This Series

The Rhetoric of Filmic Narration

by
Nick Browne

UMI RESEARCH PRESS
Ann Arbor, Michigan

Produced and distributed by
UMI Research Press
an imprint of
University Microfilms International
Ann Arbor, Michigan 48106

Library of Congress Cataloging in Publication Data

Browne, Nick.
  The rhetoric of filmic narration.

  (Studies in cinema ; no. 12)
  Revision of thesis (Ph.D.)–Harvard University, 1976.
  Bibliography: p.
  1. Moving-picture plays–History and criticism.
2. Moving-pictures–Philosophy.   I. Title. II. Title:
Filmic narration. III. Series.

PN1995.B75 1982   791.43'01'5   82-1905
ISBN 0-8357-1296-6   AACR2

To Ellen P. Wiese

Contents

Acknowledgments

Rudolf Arnheim, Christian Metz, Alfred Guzzetti, and Stanley Cavell provided in different ways the general context for this work. The Carpenter Center for the Visual Arts, Harvard University, and the Department of Visual and Environmental Studies, Louis Bakanowsky, Chairman, provided material resources and an opportunity for teaching and research. Ellen Wiese provided sustaining encouragement and critical assistance. Stella Paul, Alexandra Arendt, and Bruce McPherson helped in inestimable other ways. With appreciation to *Film Quarterly*, Chick Callenbach, Editor, for permission to reprint extended sections from two articles.

Preface

Study of the presentation of film by the act of narrating events to a spectator is different from the study of the narrative itself. This book describes the structures of filmic narration by means of detailed analysis of instances of film "texts." Because a text implies, as we show, a position for viewing, an analysis of narration calls for a study of the determinations that structure the relations among narrator, character, and spectator. Through analysis of contrasting forms of rhetoric exemplified by selected film sequences, I have outlined an approach to the analysis of filmic narration as a problem of mediation of functions. By studying particular texts in detail, and in light of a continuous theoretical interest, I propose the terms of analysis appropriate to a general study of the structure of narration in film and the spectator's experience of that structure.

Study of the way film produces and structures meaning has within the field of film study a specific contemporary context, namely the diverse research on film language. French film semiology, and in particular the writing of Christian Metz, constitutes the most systematic and influential treatment of the subject and is complex and heterogeneous enough to justify numerous studies. This book is not such a project. Rather, it is an effort to think through problems and distinctions relevant to opening the specific study of filmic narration to further systematic exploration and linking it to an analysis of filmic images. It draws upon a broad array of sources—narratology, hermeneutics, rhetoric, reader criticism, etc., principally from French, English, and Russian materials. This study is different from its sources not only in its object—film—but in emphasizing the rhetorical character of the significant determinations on and within the text.

The rhetorical approach to the study of the constitution of film texts and to the analysis of their presentation is not arbitrary, but rather is dictated as Chapter 1 shows, by the requirement of accounting system-atically for the relation of narrative, filmic imagery, and their coordinate effects. The relations between the function of the narrator, the constitution of character, and the inscription of the spectator, are treated as integral parts of a general rhetoric. The exposition of the complexity of these relations is delineated by amplifying the distinction between the level of "representation" (the level of structure that designates the relation of "address" between narrator and spectator) and the level of "story" (the level of relations among characters).

An examination of the structure and function of this general rhetoric is developed and clarified by considering two different rhetorical styles. The contrast between *Stagecoach* and *The 39 Steps* on the one hand, and Robert Bresson's *Au Hasard, Balthazar* on the other provides the basis for considering a set of specific problems having to do with describing the logic of filmic narration. What is developed in these chapters is an account of the aesthetic and discursive requirements for the (stylistically) coherent presentation of the world of the story. "Point of view" emerges as the central structuring and integrating function that determines and coordinates the multiple levels of the text and arbitrates the relation of the spectator to the text. In this respect, the book bears on a range of issues and positions in contemporary film theory.

The "text" of the various sequences that serve as the basis of the study are represented through stills and dialogue that accompany each chapter. They stand as a record of the significant features of the text and make it possible to recover for systematic scrutiny what is often either effaced by the style, not easily noticed in a natural viewing, or simply forgotten. The method of study of narratological structure through a set of still frames is linked to the role of theory in this project. The stills pose a set of textual problems and stand as evidence of claims about the relation between the tracings of action of the narrative function and the concrete rhetorical order of the text. Study of stills is a method that puts in the foreground, with critical and theoretical significance, the most particular filmic structures in relation to general narratological issues. Because the topic is narration, not narrative, analyzing short sequences provides an economical exposition of issues whose significance and form would not be materially altered by an analysis of the entire film. While blocking a sense of the impression of lifelike movement, the stills and the structures they reveal do represent significant features of the empirical reality of the text as experienced by a viewer. This is an important fact because the set of concepts—point of view, authority, narrator, character, center, view, story, representation, spectator, attention, identification, reading, etc.—that define this theory of filmic narrative attach to the signifying structure of the text as it is apprehended, though not as such, by the spectator. They constitute the terms for a general description of a rhetoric of narrative for film.

The Spectator-in-the-Text: The Rhetoric of *Stagecoach*

The sequence from John Ford's *Stagecoach* shown in the accompanying stills raises the problem of accounting for the organization of images in an instance of the "classical" fiction film and of proposing the critical terms appropriate for that account. The formal features of these images—the framing of shots and their sequencing, the repetition of set-ups, the position of characters, the direction of their glances—can be taken together as a complex structure and understood as a characteristic answer to the rhetorical problem of telling a story, of showing an action to a spectator. Because the significant relations have to do with seeing—both in the ways the characters "see" each other and the way those relations are shown to the spectator—and because their complexity and coherence can be considered as a matter of "point of view," I call the object of this study the "specular text."

Explanations of the imagery of the classical narrative film are offered by technical manuals and various theories of editing. Here, though, I wish to examine the connection between the act of narration and the imagery, specifically in the matter of the framing and the angle of view determined by set-ups, by characterizing the narrating agency or authority which can be taken to rationalize the presentation of shots. An explanation of this kind necessarily involves clarifying in some detail the notion of the "position of the spectator." Thus we must characterize the spectator's implied position with respect to the action, the way it is structured, and the specific features of the process of "reading" (though not in the sense of "interpretation"). Doing so entails a description (within the terms of the narrative) of the relation of literal and fictional space that comprehends what seems, ambiguously, like the double origin of filmic images.

An inquiry into the forms of authority for the imagery and the corresponding strategies which implicate the viewer in the action has few precedents, yet it raises general but basic questions about filmic narration that begin to clarify existing accounts of the relation of narrative to image. The sequence from *Stagecoach* is interesting as a structure precisely because, in spite of its simplicity (it has no narrative or formal eccentricity) it challenges the traditional premises of critical efforts to account for the operation and effects of "classical" film style.

The traditional rationale for the presentation of imagery is often stated by the camera's relation to the spectator. For instance, a basically dramatic account has it that the shots should show essentially what a spectator would see if the action were played on a stage, and if at each moment he had the best view of the action (thus changing angles only supply "accents"). Editing would follow the spectator's natural course of attention as it is implied by the action of the mise-en-scène. In such a mode the question of agency—that is, who is "staging" and making these events appear in this way—is referred not to the author or narrator but to the action itself, fully embodied in the characters. Everything that happens must be exhibited clearly for the eye of the spectator. On this theory, all the structures of the presentation are directed to a place external to the scene of the action—to the final authority, the ideal spectator. Oudart's recent account proposes that imagery is paradigmatically referred to the authority of the glance of the "absent one," the off-screen character within the story who in the counter shot is depicted within the frame; the spectator "identifies" with the visual field of the "owner" of the glance. The "system of the suture" is an explanation that establishes the origin of the imagery by reference to the agency of character but, surprisingly, it does not consider (indeed it seems to deny) the final agency, the authority of the narrator. The traces of the action of the narrator may seem to be effaced by this system, but such an effect can only be the result of a certain more general rhetoric. Thus I am proposing an account in which the structure of the imagery, whatever its apparent form of presentation, refers jointly to the action of an implied narrator (who defines his position with respect to the tale by his judgment) and to the imaginative action occasioned by his placing and being placed by the spectator. Neither the traditional nor the more recent theories seem fully adequate to this task.

Thus the problem that arises from *Stagecoach* is to explain the functioning of the narrator and the nature and effects of spectator placement: specifically, describing and accounting for in detail a filmic rhetoric in which the agency of the narrator in his relation to the spectator is enacted jointly by the characters and the particular sequence of shots that show them. To describe this rhetoric in a rigorous and illuminating way means clarifying in filmic terms the notions of "narrative authority," "point of view," and "reading" and showing that these concepts are of use precisely because they arise naturally from the effort to account for the concrete structures of the text.

The moment in the story that the sequence depicts is the taking of a meal at the Dry Fork station on the stage's journey to Lordsburg. Earlier in the film, the prostitute Dallas (the woman in the dark hat) has been run out of town by the Ladies' Law and Order League and has been put aboard the stagecoach. There she joined, among others, a cavalry officer's wife named Lucy (in the white hat) and Hatfield, her chivalrous but distant escort. Just before the present scene, the Ringo Kid (John Wayne), who has broken out of jail to avenge his brother's murder, has been ordered aboard by the sheriff when discovered by the side of the road. The sequence begins immediately after a vote among the members of the group to decide whether to go on to Lordsburg, and ends shortly before the end of the scene when the group exits the station. For purposes of convenience I have called shots (4), (8), and (10), which are from the same set-up, series A; and shots (3), (7), (9), and (11), series B.

One of the rationales that might be proposed to account for the set-ups, the spatial fields they show, the sequence of shots, is their relation to the "psychology" of the characters. How, if at all, are the set-ups linked to the visual attention, as with the glance, or say the interests of a character in the story? In the shot/reverse shot pattern which is sometimes, wrongly I think, taken as an exclusive paradigm of the "classical" style, the presence of the shot on the screen is "explained" or read as the depiction of the glance of the off-screen character, who, a moment later, is shown in the reverse shot. But because only a few shots of this sequence (or of most films) follow this pattern we shall be pressed to a different formulation. The general question is how the two set-ups of the two major series of shots—series A from the head of the table and series B from the left side—are to be explained.

Series A is related to the visual attention of the woman at the head of the table, Lucy. The connection between the shots and her view, especially in the modulation of the force and meaning of that view, must, however, be established. These shots from A are readable as the depiction of Lucy's glance only retrospectively, after series B has shown her at the head of the table and after the animation conveyed in the dolly forward has implied its significance. The point remains, however, that the shots of series A are finally clearly authorized by a certain disposition of attention of one of the characters.

In contrast to series A, the series B shots from the left of the table are like the opening and closing shots (1, 12) in not being associated with or justified spatially as the depiction of anyone's glance. Can the placement of these shots be justified either as the "best angle" for the spectator, or as the depiction of some other more complex conception of "psychology" of character than an act of attention in a glance? Persons to whom these shots might be attributed as views would be Dallas or the outlaw Ringo, for they satisfy one condition: they are out of the A-series frame. As series A shows, in this style the association of a shot with a glance is effected by a coincidence of geographical places, eye and camera. But here, quite plainly, neither Dallas nor Ringo are in a position to view from this angle. And in each shot, Lucy is in the frame.

To attribute the shots of series B—to justify their placement spatially to some conception of character psychology—requires some other justification than the mere representation of someone's glance. What kind of psychological account could explain the alternation of these precise framings? What kind of mental disposition, ensemble of attitude, judgment, and intention, does this framing signify? Whose disposition? On what basis would such an attribution be effected? If establishing the interpretation of the framing depended on, or was referred to, a character's "state of mind" which in fact changes significantly over the course of the sequence for each of the major characters (Dallas, Ringo, and Lucy), how would it be possible to accommodate those changing feelings to the fixity of set-up? The fact of the fixity of set-up denies that the explanation for camera placement can as a principle be referred to a psychology of character(s) based on the kind of emotional changes—surprise, repudiation, naivete, humiliation—that eventuate in the sequence.

As another hypothesis we could say that the particular compositional features of series B are a presentation not of the "mind" of any single character but of a state of affairs within the group, a relationship among the parties. What is the state of affairs within this society that the framing depicts? There are two significant features of the composition from set-up B: the relation of Lucy in the immediate foreground to the group behind her, a group whose responsiveness to events repeats the direction of her own attention, and her relation, spatially, to Dallas and Ringo who, excluded by the left edge of the frame, are outside. The permanent and underlying fact about the mise-en-scène which justifies the fixity of camera placement is its status as a social drama of alliance and antagonism between two social roles—Lucy, an insider, a married woman and defender of custom; and Dallas, an outsider and prostitute who violates the code of the table. The camera set-ups and the spatial fields they reveal, the compositional exclusion of the outlaw couple and their isolation in a separate space, with the implied assertion of Lucy's custodial relation to the body of legitimate society, respond to and depict in formal terms the social "positions" of the characters. In the kind of dramatic presentation they effect, the features of the framing are not justified as the depiction of personal psychology considered as changes of feeling; instead, by their emphasis on social positions, or types, they declare a psychology of intractable situations.

The framing of series B from the left of the table does not represent literally or figuratively any single person's view; rather, it might be said, it depicts, by what it excludes and includes, the interplay of social positions within a group. This asymmetry of social position of Lucy over Dallas extends as well to formal and compositional features of the sequence. Though set-up B represents both positions, Dallas's negatively, it makes Lucy's position privileged in the formal mechanism of narrative exposition. The fundamental narrative feature of the sequence is a modification and inflection of the logic of shot/counter shot. Here it is an alternation of series A and B around, not two characters, but either Lucy's eye or body. That is, in series A Lucy is present as an eye, as the formal beholder of the scene. Alternately, in B, Lucy is shown bodily dominating the foreground, and as the eye to which the views of series A are referred. Formally the narration proceeds by alternatingly shifting Lucy's presence from the level of the depicted action, as body (B), to the level of representation, as the invisible eye (A), making Lucy's presence the central point of spatial orientation and legibility. In shots (5) and (6), the close-up of the exchange of looks between the two women, the formal asymmetry is the difference of their frontality, and the shot of Lucy is from a place that Dallas could not literally copy. Lucy's frontality (5) marks a dispossession, a displacement, that corresponds to Dallas's social "absence" in the entire sequence—to her exclusion from the frame in B, to her isolation as the object of Lucy's scornful glance in A. By contrast to Lucy's presence everywhere, as body and eye, Dallas's eye is never taken as the source of authority for a shot. Her eye is averted. She is always, in both A and B, the object of another's gaze—a condition that corresponds to the inferiority of her social position, and to her formal invisibility—she can not authorize a view.

The shots of set-up B, which might be called "objective," or perhaps "nobody's" shots, in fact refer to or are a representation of Lucy's social dominance and formal privilege. B shows a field of vision that closely matches Lucy's *conception* of her own place in that social world: its framing corresponds to her alliance with the group and to her intention to exclude the outsiders, to deny their claim to recognition. It is in other words not exactly a description of Lucy's subjectivity but an objectification of her social self-conception. Though Lucy is visible in the frame, series B might be said, metaphorically, to embody her point of view.

This explanation seems cogent as far as it goes. But there are some further issues that arise from the passage, in the way it is experienced, that suggest that the foregoing analysis of the justification of these formal features is incomplete as an account of the grounds for the effects the passage produces, and theoretically limited in terms of explaining the strategies of framing and other premises of the narration.

Simply put, the experience of this passage is a feeling of empathy for Dallas's exclusion and humiliation, and a repudiation of Lucy's prejudice as unjust, two feelings brought together by a sense of inevitability of the conflict. There is in other words a curious opposition between the empathetic response of a spectator toward Dallas with the underlying premises of the mechanism of the narrative which are so closely related, formally, to Lucy's presence, point of view, and interests. It is this sense of incongruity between feeling and formal structure that occasions the following effort to consider the sequence in terms of the ways it produces its effects, that is, rhetorically.

One question about a formal matter, which draws attention to the limitations of a structural account based on a conception of the social order, is why the outsiders are seen from a position that is associated with Lucy's place at the table, her gaze. This fact, and the action of the audience within the film, casts doubt on two theories of agency. Our attention as spectators, in the shots of series B, does not follow the visual attention of any depicted characters. These shots might perhaps be read as statements of the "interests" of characters, the nature of their social positions, but that is already a kind of commentary or interpretation that needs explanation. The actions of the men at the bar, the audience within the film, disprove the traditional rationale for editing stated by reference to an ideal spectator: as "placed" spectators we anticipate, not follow, the movements of their attention (2, 3); the object of their attention is sometimes out of the frame we see (3b) and what they see is shown only from a view significantly different from any simply "accented" of "best view," indeed from a place they could not occupy; and sometimes (7b, 8) they have turned away, uninterested, but the screen doesn't go black. In general, an adequate account of the formal choices of the passage must be quite different from an account of the event as if it were staged for the natural attention of a spectator, depicted or real. To ask why the spectator sees in the way he does refers to a set of premises distinguishable from an account based on the attention of either a character or an ideal spectator. It refers to the concrete logic of the placement of the implied spectator and to the theory of presentation that accounts for the shaping of his response. Such an account makes the "position" of the spectator, the way in which he is implicated in the scene, the manner and location of his presence, his point of view, problematical.

It is this notion of the "position of the spectator" that I wish to clarify insofar as that notion illuminates the rhetorical strategies, particularly choice of set-up (implying scale and framing) that depicts the action. In contemporary French film theory, particularly in the work of Comolli and Baudry, the notion of the "place" of the spectator is derived from the central position of the eye in perspective and photographic representation. By literally substituting the epistemological subject, the spectator, for the eye in an argument about filmic representation, the filmic spectator is said to be "theological," and "centered" with respect to filmic images. Thus the theory of the filmic spectator is treated as if subject to the Derridian critique of center, presence, etc. French theory is wrong to enforce this analogy based on the position of the eye in photographic perspective, because what is optical and literal in that case corresponds only to the literal place of the spectator in the projection hall, and not at all to his figurative place in the film, nor to his place as subject to the rhetoric of the film, or reader or producer of the sense of the discourse. Outside of a French ideological project which fails to discriminate literal and figurative space, the notion of "place" of the spectator, and of "center," is an altogether problematic notion whose significance and function in critical discussion has yet to be explicated.

The sequence from *Stagecoach* provides the terms in which the notion of the position of the spectator might be clarified, provided we distinguish, without yet expecting full clarification, the different senses of "position." A spectator is (a) seated physically in the space of the projection hall and (b) placed by the camera in a certain fictional position with respect to the depicted action; moreover (c), insofar as we see from what we might take to be the eye of a character, we are invited to occupy the place allied to the place he holds in, for example, the social system; and finally (d) in another figurative sense of place, it is the only way that our response can be accounted for, we can identify with a character's position in a certain situation.

In terms of the passage at hand, the question is then: how can I describe my "position" as spectator in identifying with the humiliated position of one of the depicted characters, Dallas, when my views of her belong to those of another, fictional character, Lucy, who is in the act of rejecting her? What is the spectator's "position" in identifying with Dallas in the role of the passive character? Dallas in averting her eyes from Lucy's in shot (6) accepts a view of herself in this encounter as "prostitute" and is shamed. However, in identifying with Dallas in the role of outcast, presumably the basis for the evocation of our sympathy and pity, our response as spectator is not one of shame, or anything even analogous. We do not suffer or repeat the humiliation. I understand Dallas's feeling but I am not so identified with her that I reenact it. One of the reasons for this restraint is that though I identify with Dallas's abject position of being seen as an unworthy object by someone whose judgment she accepts, I identify with her as the object of another's action. Indeed, in a remarkable strategy, I am asked to see Dallas through Lucy's eyes. That as spectator I am sharing Lucy's view and, just as importantly, her manner of viewing, is insisted on most emphatically by the dolly forward (4) and by disclosures effected by shot/counter shot, thus placing us in a lively and implicated way in a position fully associated with Lucy's place at the head of the table.

Insofar as I identify with Dallas, it is not by repeating her shame, but by imagining myself in her position (situation). The early scenes of the film have carefully prepared us to believe that this exclusion is an unjust act. When the climactic moment arrives, our identification with Dallas as an object of view is simultaneously established as the ground for repudiating the one whose view we share and are implicated in. Though I share Lucy's literal geographical position of viewing at this moment in the film, I am not committed to her figurative point of view. I can, in other words, repudiate Lucy's view of or judgment on Dallas, without negating it as a view, in a way that Dallas herself, captive of the other's image, cannot. Because our feelings as spectators are not "analogous" to the interests and feelings of the characters, we are not bound to accept their views either of themselves or of others. Our "position as spectator" then is very different from the previous senses of "position": it is defined neither in terms of orientation within the constructed geography of the fiction, nor of social position of the viewing character. On the contrary, our point of view on the sequence is tied more closely to our attitude of approval or disapproval and is very different from any literal viewing angle or character's point of view.

Identification asks us as spectators to be two places at once, where the camera is and "with" the depicted person—thus its double structure of viewer/viewed. As a powerful emotional process it thus throws into question any account of the position of the spectator as centered at a single point or at the center of any simply optical system. This passage shows that identification necessarily has a double structure in the way it implicates the spectator in both the position of the one seeing and the one seen. This sequence, however, does establish a certain kind of "center" in the person of Lucy. Each of the shots is referred alternatingly to the scene before her eye, or the scene of her body, but it is a "center" that functions as a principle of spatial legibility, and is associated with a literal point within the constructured space of the fiction. This center stands, though, as I have suggested, in a very complicated relation to our "position" as spectator. That is, the experience of the passage shows that our identification, in the Freudian sense of an emotional investment, is not with the center, either Lucy or the camera. Rather, if, cautiously, we can describe our figurative relation to a film in geographical terms, of "in," "there," "here," "distance," (and this sequence, as part of its strategy as a fiction, explicitly asks us to by presenting action to us from the literal view of a character) then as spectators, we might be said to formally occupy someone else's place, to be "in" the film, all the while being "outside" it in our seats. We can identify with a character and share her "point of view" even if the logic of the framing and selection of shots of the sequence deny that she has a view or a place within the society that the mise-en-scène depicts. There are significant differences between structures of shots, views, and identification: indeed, this sequence has shown, as a principle, that we do not "identify" with the camera but with the characters, and hence, contrary to Oudart's theory, do not feel dispossessed by a change in shots. For a spectator, as distinct perhaps from a character, point of view is not definitively or summarily stated by any single shot or even set of shots from a given spatial location.

The way in which we as spectators are implicated in the action is as much a matter of our position with respect to the unfolding of those events in time as in their representation from a point in space. The effect of the mode of sequencing, the regular opposition of insiders and outsiders, is modulated in ways that shape the attitudes of the spectator/reader toward the action. This durational aspect emphasizes the process of inhabiting a text with its rhythms of involvement and disengagement in the action, and suggests that the spectator's position, his being in time, might appropriately be designated the "reader-in-the-text." His doubly structured position of identification with the features and force of the act of viewing and with the object in the field of vision, are the visual terms of the dialectic of spectator placement. The rhetorical effort of shots (2–6) is directed to establishing the connection between shots and a "view," to endowing the position at the head of the table with a particular sense of personalized glance. Shot (2), like (4), cannot at the moment it appears on the screen be associated with Lucy's glance. The shot/counter shot sequencing discloses Lucy's location, and the turn of the head (3b) establishes a spatial relation between A and B; the animation, or gesture, implied by the dolly forward, combined with the emotional intensity implied by the choice of scale (5, 6) are read in terms of a personalized agency and clarified by what is shown in the visible field, Lucy's stern face (5). It is a rhetoric that unites the unfolding shots and gives meaning to this depicted glance-affront. It creates with the discrete shots (2, 3, 4) the impression of a coherent act of viewing, a mental unity whose meaning must make itself felt by the viewer at the moment of confrontation (5, 6) to effect the sense of repudiation of Lucy's view and the abjectness of Dallas. It takes time—a sequence of shots, in other words—to convey and specify the meaning of an act of viewing.

Reading, as this instance shows, is in part a process of retrospection, situating what could not be "placed" at the moment of its origin and bringing it forward to an interpretation of the meaning of the present moment. As such it has a complex relation to the action and to the spatial location of viewing. But the process of reading also depends on forgetting. After the climactic moment (5, 6) signalled by Dallas's averting her eyes, a different temporal strategy is in effect. Lucy has looked away in (7b) and in subsequent shots from the head of the table, our attention is directed not so much to the act of showing, and what it means—unawareness (2), recognition (4), rejection (6)—but rather in (8) and (10) is directed at the action within the frame. The spectator's forgetting of what the dramatic impact depended on just a few moments before (here the personalized force that accompanied the act of showing the shot as a glance) is an effect of placement that depends on an experience of duration which occludes a previous significance and replaces it with another, a process we might call fading.

The modulation of the effects of fading are what, to take another example, is at issue in the interpretation of the shots of both series A and B. I have argued above that the set-up and field of B correspond to Lucy's understanding of her place in the social system—to her point of view in the metaphorical sense. This interpretation corresponds to the general impression of the first six shots, taken together, as representing Lucy's manner of seeing. Shot (7) initiates a new line of dramatic action that poses the question of what Lucy will do now, and also begins a process not exactly of re-reading, but a search for a new reading of the meaning of the set-ups. At this moment (7b), Lucy has turned her attention away from Dallas and is now turned toward Hatfield; and Ringo, previously occupied with his table etiquette (2, 4) is looking (8b, 10) intently out of frame right. The initial sense of the set-up B is partially replaced by, but coexists with another: that the depicted action in the frame is now being viewed by someone looking from outside the frame, namely Ringo, who is waiting expectantly for something to happen. The view from the left of the table is readable, not exactly as Lucy's self-conception as before, and not as a depiction of Ringo's glance, but as a representation of his interest in the scene, his point of view (again in the metaphorical sense). Similarly shots (8) and (10), showing Dallas and Ringo, no longer seem to characterize Lucy as the one doing the seeing, as in (4) and (6); they have become impersonal. The rigidity and opposition of set-ups A and B correspond to the rigidity of social position, but our reading of the changing secondary significances of the framing is an effect of fading that is responsive to acts of attention and seeing depicted within the frame.

Our anticipation, our waiting to see what will happen, is provoked and represented on the level of the action by the turning around of the audience-in-the-film (Billy and Doc Boone in 3b, 9). Our own feeling, because of our visual place to the left of the table, is closer to Ringo's than to theirs. Certainly the distention and delay of the climactic moment by the virtual repetition (9, 11a) of those shots of a hesitating Lucy (unnecessary for simple exposition) produce a sense of our temporal identification with Ringo (8b, 10), necessary for the success of the moment as drama—its uncertainty and resolution. The drama depends for the lesson it demonstrates not on Lucy's self-regard before a general public as previously, but on being watched by the parties to be affected. It is Ringo's increasingly involved presence as an authority for a view, even though he mistakenly thinks he is being ostracized, that makes the absent place left by Lucy's departure so evidently intended as a lesson in manners, so accusingly empty. By these strategies and effects of duration—retrospection, fading, delay, and anticipation—the reading of emphasis on the act of showing or what is shown, the significance of angle and framing, can be modulated. Together these means define features of a rhetoric which, though different from the placement effected by visual structures, also locate and implicate the reader/spectator in the text.

The spectator's place, the locus around which the spatial/temporal structures of presentation are organized, is a construction of the text which is ultimately the product of the narrator's disposition toward the tale. Such structures, which in shaping and presenting the action, prompt a manner and indeed a path of reading, convey and are closely allied to the guiding moral commentary of the film. In this sequence the author has effaced himself, as in other instances of indirect discourse, for the sake of the characters and the action. Certainly he is nowhere visible in the same manner as the characters. Rather he is visible only through the materialization of the scene and in certain masked traces of his action. The indirect presence to his audience that the narrator enacts, the particular form of self-effacement, could be described as the masked displacement of his narrative authority as the producer of imagery from himself to the agency of his characters. That is, the film makes it appear as though it were the depicted characters to whom the authority for the presentation of shots can be referred—most evidently in the case of a depiction of a glance, but also, in more complex fashion, in the reading of shots as depictions of a "state of mind." The explanation of the presence of the imagery is referred by the film not to the originating authority who stands invisible, behind the action, but to his masks within the depicted scene.

In accord with the narrator's efforts to direct attention away from his own activity, to mask and displace it, the narrator of *Stagecoach* has a visible persona, Lucy, perform a significant formal function in the narration: to constitute and to make legible and continuous the depicted space, by referring shots on the screen alternately to the authority of her eye or the place of her body. The literal place of the spectator in the projection hall, where in a sense all the shots are directed, is a "center" that has a figurative correspondence on the level of the discourse in the "place" that Lucy occupies in the depicted space. But because Lucy performs her integrative function not exactly by her being at a place, the head of the table, but by enacting a kind of central consciousness that corresponds to a social and formal role, a role which for narrative purposes can be exploited by shifting the views representing the manner of her presence, the notion of "center" might be thought of not as a geographical place, but as a structure or function. As such, this locus makes it possible for the reader himself to occupy that role and to make the depicted space coherent and readable. For the spectator, the "center" is not just a point either in the projection hall or in the depicted geography, but is the result of the impression produced by the functioning of the narrative and of his being able to fictionally occupy the absent place.

Locating this function, "inscribing" the spectator's place on the level of the depicted action, has the effect of making the story seem to tell itself by reference not to an outside author but to a continuously visible, internal narrative authority. This governing strategy, of seeming to internalize the source of the exposition in characters, and thus of directing the spectator's attention to the depicted action, is supported by other features of the style: shot/counter shot, matching of glances, continuity.

Consequently, the place of the spectator in his relation to the narrator is established by, though not limited to, identifications with characters and the views they have of each other. More specifically his "place" is defined through the variable force of identification with the one viewing and the one viewed—as illustrated in the encounter between Lucy and Dallas. Though the spectator may be placed in the "center" by the formal function Lucy performs, he is not committed to her view of things. On the contrary, in the context of the film, that view is instantly regarded as insupportable. Our response to Dallas supports the sense that the spectator's figurative position is not stated by a description of where the camera is in the geography of the scene. On the contrary, though the spectator's position is closely tied to the fortunes and views of the characters, our analysis suggests that identification, in the original sense of an emotional bond, need not be with the character whose view he shares, even less with the disembodied camera. Evidently, a spectator is several places at once—with the fictional viewer, with the viewed, and at the same time in a position to evaluate and respond to the claims of each. This fact suggests that like the dreamer, the filmic spectator is a plural subject: in his reading he is and is not himself.

In a film, imagining ourselves in a character's place by identification, in respect to the actual situation, is a different process, indeed a different order of fiction than taking a shot as originating from a certain point within the fictional geography. The relation though between the literal space of the projection hall and the depicted space of the film image is continuously problematic for a definition of the "thatness" of the screen and for an account of the place of the spectator. If a discourse carries a certain impression of reality it is an effect not exactly of the image, but rather of the way the image is placed by the narrative or argument. My relation to an image on the screen is literal because it can be taken as being directed to a physical point, my seat (changing that seat doesn't alter my viewing angle on the action), as though I were the fixed origin of the view. On the other hand, the image can also be taken as originating from a point in a different kind of space, recognizably different in terms of habitability from that of the projection hall: it is from a fictional and changeable place implied by an origin contained in the image. The filmic image thus implies the ambiguity of a double origin—from both my literal place as spectator and from the place where the camera is within the imaginative space.

One structural result of the ambiguous relation of literal and depicted space and of the seemingly contradictory efforts of the text to both place and displace the spectator is the prohibition against the "meeting," though no such act is literally possible, of actor's and spectator's glances, a prohibition that is an integral feature of the sequence as a "specular text." In its effect on the spectator, the prohibition defines the different spaces he simultaneously inhabits before the screen. By denying his presence in one sense, the prohibition establishes a boundary at the screen that underscores the fact that the spectator can have no actual physical exchange with the depicted world, that he can do nothing relevant to change the course of the action. It places him irretrievably outside the action.

At the same time, the prohibition is the initial premise of a narrative system for the representation of fictional space and the means of introducing the spectator imaginatively into it. The prohibition effects this construction and engagement by creating an obliquity between our angle of viewing and that of the characters which works to make differences of angle and scale readable as representations of different points of view. As such it plays a central part in our process of identification or nonidentification with the camera and depicted characters. It provides the author an ensemble of narrative forms—an imaginary currency consisting of temporary exchange, substitution, and identification—that enables us, fictionally, to take the place of another, to inhabit the text as a reader.

Establishing agency either by the authority of character or of spectator corresponds in its alternative rhetorical forms to the articulation of the ambiguity of the double origin of the image. In a particular text it is the narration that establishes and arbitrates the spectator's placement between these two spaces. *Stagecoach* makes definite efforts to imply that not only is the spectator not there, not present in his seat, but that the film-object originates from an authority within the fictional space. The narration seems to insist that the film is a freestanding entity which a spectator, irrelevant finally to its construction, could only look on from the outside. On the other hand, in the ways that I have described, the film is directed in all its structures of presentation toward the narrator's construction of a commentary on the story and toward placing the spectator at a certain "angle" to it. The film has tried not just to direct the attention, but to place the eye of the spectator inside the fictional space, to make his presence integral and constitutive of the structure of views. The explanation the film seems to give of the action of narrative authority is a denial of the existence of a narrator different from character and an affirmation of the dominating role of fictional space. It is a spatial mode not determined by the ontology of the image as such but is in the last instance an effect of the narration.

Masking and displacement of narrative authority are thus integral to establishing the sense of the spectator "in" the text, and the prohibition to establishing the film as an independent fiction, different from dream in being the product of another, that can nevertheless be in-habited. Fascination by identification with character is a way the integrity of fictional space is validated and because the spectator occupies a fictional role, is a way too that the film can efface the spectator's consciousness of his position. As a production of the spectator's reading, the sense of reality that the film enacts, the "impression of the real," protects the account the text seems to give of the absent narrator.

The cumulative effect of the narrator's strategy of placement of the spectator from moment to moment is his introduction into what might be called the moral order of the text. That is, the presentational structures which shape the action both convey a point of view and define the course of the reading, and are fundamental to the exposition of moral ideas—specifically a discussion about the relation of insiders to outsiders. The effect of the distinction between pure and impure is the point of the sequence, though as a theme it is just part of the total exposition. The sequence thus assists in the construction of attitudes toward law and custom and to those who live outside their strictures. It introduces the question of the exercise of social and customary (as distinguished from legal) authority. To the extent we identify with Ringo and Dallas—and the film continuously invites us to by providing multiple grounds: the conventional order and the morality it enforces is put in doubt. Without offering a full interpretation of the theme of *Stagecoach* which I think would be connected with the unorthodox nature of their love and the issue of Ringo's revenge and final exemption from the law by the sheriff, I can still characterize the spectator's position at this particular moment in the film.

It amounts to this, that though we see the action from Lucy's eyes and are invited by a set of structures and strategies to experience the force and character of that view, we are put in the position finally of having to reject it as a view that is right or that we could be committed to. The sequence engages us on this point through effecting an identification with a situation in which the outsider is wronged and thus that challenges Lucy's position as the agent of an intolerant authority. We are asked, by the manner in which we must read, by the posture we must adopt, to repudiate Lucy's view, to see behind the moral convention that supports intolerance, to break out of a role that may be confining us. As such, the importance of the sequence in the entire film is the way it allies us emotionally with the interests and fortunes of the outsiders as against social custom, an identification and theme that, modulated in subsequent events, continues to the end of the film. The passage, lifted out of its context, but drawing on dispositions established in previous sequences, is an illustration of the process of constructing a spectator's attitudes in the film as a whole through the control of point of view. Whether or not the Western genre can in general be characterized by a certain mode of identification, as for example in the disposition or wish to see the right done, and whether *Stagecoach* has a particularly significant place in the history of the genre by virtue of its treatment of outsiders, is an open question. In any case the reader's position is constituted by a set of views, identifications, and judgment that establish his place in the moral order of the text.

Like the absent narrator who discloses himself and makes judgment from a position inseparable from the sequence of depicted events that constitute the narrative, the spectator, in following the story, in being subject of and to the spatial and temporal placement and effects of exposition, is in the process of realizing an identity we have called his position. Following the trajectory of identifications that establishes the structure of values of a text, "reading" as a temporal process could be said to continuously reconstruct the place of the narrator and his implied commentary on the scene. In this light, reading, as distinct from interpretation, might be characterized as a guided and prompted performance that (to the extent a text allows it, and I believe *Stagecoach* does) recreates the point of view enacted in a scene. As a correlative of narration, reading could be said to be the process or reenactment by fictionally occupying the place of the narrator.

Features of the imagery—framing, sequencing, the prohibition, continuity—are associated with a rhetorical function. That is, the terms appropriate to the description of their determinations and effects refer to the narrator's action of placing an implied spectator at a certain "angle," figuratively speaking, to the story. What this sequence shows in particular is that the camera location in the fictional geography does not necessarily correspond to or explain an emotional analogy with characters in the scene. It shows the importance of distinguishing between a glance, the view of a character, the location of the camera, and the point of view of the film. The position of the implied spectator is a construction of the text linked to the vantage point from which the meaning of the story can be appreciated. As such, accounting for the problem of the formal organization and significance of filmic imagery is related to a rhetorical context and to the action of the implied narrator.

Appendix A

Stills and Dialogue from *Stagecoach*

1

RINGO. Set down here, ma'am.

2

3a

3b

DALLAS. Thank you.

4a

4b

4c

5

6a

6b

7a

7b

8a

8b

HATFIELD. May I find you another place
Mrs. Mallory? It's cooler by the window.

9

10

LUCY. Thank you.

11a

11b

11c

12a

12b

Representation and Story:
Significance in *The 39 Steps*

It is of course the narrator who exhibits the images of the film. But unlike the characters, he does not appear as such in the film. His presence is realized in another mode, that of his narrative agency. Though self-effacing, one structural sign of his action is the construction of the vantage point, continuously articulated in the text, from which the story is to be seen, a position we have called the "implied spectator." I have stated in Chapter 1 that the features of framing and sequencing are directed to and define a position with relation to the characters distinguishable from that of any character or an ideal spectator. What emerges then is the concept of narrator as the agency who makes the "point of view" of the text. This agency is implied by creating a vantage point on the action through the showing of certain images in a particular way. The concept of the narrator's point of view in the text has a direct bearing on an account of film's mode of narration and on its relation to concrete features of the imagery.

Central to continuing and elaborating the description of filmic narration begun in Chapter 1 through an analysis of the position of the spectator, is a clarification and exposition of the sphere of action, the agency, of the narrator-in-the-text. The first chapter described his functioning in rhetorical terms as surrogation, an apparent attribution of the authority for originating shots from himself to characters in order to mask his own activity. But the function of surrogation that defined a formal center of spatial legibility in the character of Lucy does not account for the role or effect or location of the narrator's "point of view." This disjuncture suggests that the agency that structures surrogation, however it is apprehended by the spectator, reserves the power to comment on the mechanism of exposition. I am suggesting that to describe film's means of narration, and production of meaning, requires a careful delineation of the difference between the roles of the implied narrator and character (and the difference between character and spectator). It calls for an analysis of the structure and the organization of two integrated but different functions.

The passage from Hitchcock's well-known thriller, *The 39 Steps*, represented here by the accompanying stills and dialogue, provides an opportunity for an examination of the role of the implied narrator through such a delineation. I consider framing and sequencing of the images and sounds that constitute this passage as evidence, as in *Stagecoach*, of the distinction between the implied spectator and character, but also, and most importantly in this chapter, of the difference between character and the agency of the implied narrator. In terms of the scope of action, I acknowledge the correspondence, well established in the critical literature, of the level of "representation" with the narrator, and the level of "story" with character. "Representation" designates the level of structure through which the narrator presents the story to the reader, and "story," the continuous line of action of the characters among themselves. The story, the "narrative object," that which is told, consists of the actions and perceptions of the characters. In terms of discourse, it is worth pointing out that characters' perceptions exist on the same level as their actions. Both are narrative objects to be depicted. In the passage at hand, the ways the characters see and respond to each other and the presence of a newspaper constitute the events of the story: exposure, recognition, misperception. The central concern in this chapter, though, is an analysis of the representation, of the mode by which the narrator structures and interprets the story to the spectator. By the specific cinematic features of framing and sequencing the action, he both characterizes and at the same time distances himself from the figures in a way that defines the scope of the symbolic action, the commentary, what I am calling "point of view." I wish in other words to analyze the basic structure of filmic narration, a form of surrogation, as a dialogue between structures of analogy and independence, between views *of* and views *on* character. Specifically, by considering in detail the function of the moving camera and the depiction of acts of character's misperception, this chapter will define the nature of filmic representation as the production of an interpretation (on a "signifying object," the "story," that exists in its own sphere). Essentially, the narrator makes sense by interpreting the experience of the character. His task is both to exhibit and comment on it. Representation, the passage shows, is not restricted to narrative, but also includes symbolization. The narrative action of authority-in-the-text is a mode of showing that exhibits and discloses meaning. It is a commentary on the views and conflict of views of the characters. As such, the power of this agency is closely associated with its capacity for movement in space and tied therefore to the method of this essay, the study of still frames. This study of the relation between the two levels of discourse in Hitchcock, representation and story, begins an account of the role of the narrator's point of view in the production and the reader's apprehension of the meaning of the filmic narrative.

In its essential events, the "story" is constituted by the ways the characters see, do not see, or misunderstand the significance of a newspaper. The hero, Hannay, is in a predicament. To understand his position in this scene, we must appreciate the situation the film puts him in. Hannay is a Canadian visiting England. Anabel, a woman who tells him of an espionage ring, is murdered by foreign agents in his apartment. Because of the spy-thriller circumstances of the murder, foreign agents trying to smuggle an important state secret out of the country, Hannay decides he would not be believed by the police and that the only way to clear himself is to expose the machinations of the spy ring. Following a few cryptic clues, he takes the train to Scotland to begin his search for the man, mentioned by Anabel, who he presumes is a friend. The police do believe he is guilty and have begun to close in. Hannay is forced by their search of the train to escape and continue on foot. When the scene under discussion begins, Hannay comes upon the Crofter at dusk and on the pretense of looking for work as a motor mechanic, stops to ask for information. The Crofter agrees for a small sum to lodge Hannay for the night.

Underlying the dramatic complication that eventuates in the sequence is a traditional joke—the story of the traveling salesman and the farmer's daughter. The young woman Hannay finds in the Crofter's house is really the Crofter's wife, though young enough to be his daughter, and at first, Hannay thinks she is. The stranger's arrival on the farm creates a situation which in a short time is no joking matter.

The events of the narrative are initiated by Hannay's wish to see the newspaper. The acts of perception, the frustrations and consequences, are linked to his effort to read and to hide it. We are asked to believe that the newspaper is tantamount, on the level of the story, to Hannay's identity. Discovery by other characters means the exposure of his false identity, not Hannay as mechanic, but Hannay as murderer, or as seducer. The action of the story itself has two aspects: movement and perception. On one level is the entirely inadvertent action of physically placing and replacing the newspaper to make it inaccessible, then accessible to Hannay, and then so it can be seen by Margaret. Margaret acts to delay Hannay's reading, first by her presence (6a), and then by moving the newspaper from table to counter (6c). The husband's entrance distracts Margaret and allows Hannay to read the paper. But it is the husband's order ("Put down the paper") that causes Hannay to put it back on the table where it is seen, uncovered, by Margaret. The wife functions in other words to prevent Hannay's reading, the husband to effect it, and Hannay to effect Margaret's recognition. In a similar way, Margaret's inadvertent act of uncovering the paper (8) causes Hannay to approach her

(9b), a situation that when the husband enters and sees them, is the basis of his suspicion and of his consequent action. Action on the first level is a kind of free play of functions. That is, changing agents is possible without changing the result. Margaret, for example, could light the lamp. But on the second level of story, the perceptual, the manner of seeing Hannay's efforts to read the newspaper is rigorously specified. It constitutes the significant action—understanding or misunderstanding—and defines the concrete meaning of character. For Hannay, of course, who is the only one of the characters who understands the actual significance of his situation, the object of his furtive glance is the half-hidden paper. Margaret, screened from Hannay's efforts by the cabinet door, is oblivious to his concern. What exposes him to danger, we are asked to believe, is that literal exposure of the paper by removing the packages, or too obvious an interest in the paper if seen by others, constitutes a threat against his false identity as Hannay-mechanic. Thus he attempts to hide and disguise his efforts to see. In sum, the structural organization of the level of the story consists of double but interlocked set of elements, action and perception, with different degrees of necessity, articulated on the dramatic premise that makes seeing and the threat of seeing the important events. The narration functions to integrate circulation and placement of the paper with the forms of perception of character: the levels are linked, but always to signify the importance of perception.

The "representation" consists of showing these actions, the "narrative object," to the spectator. It structures the imagery through the ways, guilty or innocent, Hannay is seen by wife, husband, and by us. It is a way of describing the position and function of the narrator-in-the-text.

The rhetoric of the passage articulates the differences between what the spectator knows of Hannay's position and what the characters know. It makes them essential events. It defines the action as exposure, recognition, misperception, as Hannay is seen as endangered innocent, as murderer, or as seducer. What is at stake in the film is Hannay's exposure as the Portland Place murderer, his guilt or innocence, and we see that the character's actions are to be judged by this standard. These forms of perception are made significant by the way the film establishes a relationship between Hannay and ourselves.

The composition of the master shot (set-up 4) is laid out in three receding zones—packages/Hannay/Margaret. By masking Hannay's action from Margaret in the depth of the frame (6a), this composition creates the sense of a unique and private vantage point: only we see his furtive search. It encourages us to experience, like Hannay, being endangered and discovered, and creates a sense of alliance that Margaret's approach threatens. The spectator is set up to be implicated in Hannay's position even before he knows what it is. (4a) places us before the table with the packages prominently displayed in the foreground, just as Hannay enters the frame. This spatial organization anticipates any character's comprehension of its possible meaning, making us the sole witness to what we will come to see as Hannay's discovery. The set-up creates and exploits for dramatic effect, the difference between his position and ours and at the same time prepares us to identify with it. Hannay's self-consciously guilty actions establish the stakes. By the composition the spectator is aware of the importance of an undefined something, even before Hannay, but the exact specification of what, is filled in as "newspaper" only by Hannay's mediation (5). From the first our knowledge of and interest in the paper is mediated by Hannay's attention. By analogy of scale, downward angle, the spectator seems to occupy Hannay's subjective vantage point on the paper, though the image we see (5) is from a position to the front of the table, a position that he does not in fact occupy. Such an analogy of viewpoints does not depend on an exact spatial correspondence, but is an effect of rhetoric accomplished by a conventional syntax, whose point is both to depict his view and to create the sense that we share it. We are in a position that corresponds to his own: unreadability of the paper for us means unreadability for him.

The difference between our position and Hannay's (between 4a and 4b), amounts to a momentary superiority of knowledge by the way it anticipates and leaves open a "significance-for-character" to come into being. As a sign of the authority of the narration, this difference tends though to be effaced in the rest of the passage by strategies that establish, through versions of centering, an analogy of motivation between Hannay's interests and the imagery. This strategy makes the imagery intelligible in terms of the way Hannay experiences the situation of frustration and endangerment. Because our view of the paper has been identified with Hannay's as being incomplete and yet significant, we are inclined to be identified with his frustration over its removal. Its uncovering makes his position all the more precarious. Though the master set-up (of 4, 5, 6, 7) is perpendicular and at a distance from Hannay's position at the table, it is nevertheless a representation of his point of view. The panning of the camera (6, 7) both establishes and makes reference to his centered position and shifting acts of attention. By depicting the uneventful business of Margaret's cooking, and by the delay they introduce, those movements create a sense of distention of time as a preoccupied Hannay might experience it. This experience of interruption and delay created by the alternating left and right sweep of the camera, which while traversing Hannay's place at the table, sometimes leaves him out, is effected by the fixed location of the camera. That is, the fixed place of the camera which defines the "center," acts for us as a reminder of his continuing anxiety and concern. The panning creates and measures by its incidental description the sense of delay that corresponds to the secondary object of his attention—her movements. The camera movements thus depict

Hannay's concern by recreating in us an image of his subjective experience. In this way, by actions of the camera that seem to imitate those of the character, the narration can create a sense of emotional identification and of viewpoint by formal means, even if the camera is facing him.

The husband's seeing is also an object of depiction. The object of the Crofter's attention though is Hannay, specifically Hannay's effort to read the paper and to cope with Margaret's recognition. In this way, the issue of Hannay's identity (as implied by the headlines) is articulated and enmeshed in another perceptual structure, that of the husband's misunderstanding. The husband's exits (1b, 23c) and entrance (10b), a matter of abandoning or retaking his place as husband, or as master of the house, articulate the framework for the action of (mis)perception. His position as titular authority, a place marked compositionally and psychologically by his standing between Margaret and Hannay (2a, 15b), is challenged by the stranger's entrance and the triangular situation that emerges. To Hannay's question "Your daughter?" he snaps "My wife," but walks away.

The husband's unexpected return from outside the house (10b) changes our understanding of the danger Hannay faces. Until now (4–9) we have been engaged in his frustrated efforts to see the paper. At the critical point when Margaret uncovers it, Hannay tries to distract her (9), but the object of his attention is behind her. His movement and his effort at distraction, flattery, put them in a position of potential intimacy that Margaret tacitly recognizes when she invokes her husband's disapproval of the topics of conversation—city life and her attractiveness. The husband's entrance constitutes an interruption of our initial interest just as it surprises them. But we, unlike the characters, see the Crofter come silently through the door (10a) and by this privileged view, anticipate the reaction of the couple.

The husband's viewpoint (10b, 11a, b, c) is depicted so that we are explicitly aware that it is his. His head comes into the frame left (11a) as if to take possession of the shot (11b). At first he is hardly visible, his face turned toward the couple, but soon he fills the immediate foreground. It is the couple who is in focus. The sense of the personalization of a view is articulated by a tracking movement of the camera that exactly corresponds, for a moment, with his walking. The reverse shot of the couple (11a)—they are looking almost directly into the camera—is thus understood immediately as the field being seen by the husband. That is, as the Crofter moves into the frame, and the side of his darkened face appears, the two shots (10b, 11a) are seen in syntactical combination. The menacing face of the husband in (10b) is understood, as the face, turned away from us, that they see (11a). The second shot shows their visible response, shock and apprehension, and describes the way they interpret that view. The shot with them all in the frame is a summary of the action: it depicts his view of them, shows their view of and response to him, and locates the spectator, with the husband, but having an independent view of the entire exchange as an object.

There is a broader rhetorical context to this exchange. Through the husband's surmises (in 11), the previous action and conversation between Hannay and Margaret (9b) is seen by the spectator in a new way. The husband sees and judges the situation before him by the compromised physical position of the couple and from overhearing Margaret's remark to Hannay, "You ought not to say that." Knowing nothing of Hannay's efforts to see the newspaper and already suspicious of and unsettled by the inherently romantic situation of his wife with a younger man, he interprets Hannay's attempt to distract Margaret in his own way—with suspicion. His and our interpretations of the meaning of Hannay and Margaret's closeness begin both to converge and to conflict. Our previous understanding of the apparently innocent action of Hannay's trying to see the paper was, we discover, from a potentially incriminating point of view. Shock resulting from the intervention of a new superimposed structure of perception defined by the husband's suspicion, displaces the initial sense and gives rise to a second and transforming meaning: sexual complicity. The narrator gives us a viewpoint on the action (9b) which, until the husband appeared, was only virtual, and which originally we could not have sustained, but are now implicated in. We are put in the position, different from any of the characters, of appreciating this ambiguity of interpretation by recognizing that the husband's suspicion, though founded on a misperception, is not entirely without foundation. As long as the husband occupies the frame, our innocent view is suspended, replaced by one that sees the couple as guilty. The Crofter's passing out of the frame, while confirming that what we have seen was his view, does not restore our initial innocence. What establishes this image as his, and discriminates it from ours is the stopping of the camera with whose tracking motion and field of view we were identified. The narrator's bringing the camera to a halt allows the Crofter to pass out of the frame and deflects our attention from the camera motion per se to the depicted scene. In this moment, what we see depicted is the limitations of the Crofter's view—his misperception. The Crofter re-enters the frame in the same shot, a moment later (11c). This marks a change of function, from agent on the level of the representation to agent on the level of the story (he lights the lamp). The same transformation masks the moment (11b) when the formal "center" shifts from Hannay to the Crofter.

Later, at the table, in his ignorance of the true cause of their secret communication, the Crofter's suspicious surveying of their exchange of looks gives further grounds for his assuming a romantic intrigue. He hypocritically interrupts his praying ("... to turn our heart from wicked- ness ...") to suspiciously survey the scene with a view that construes the ambiguous evidence of their communication as betrayal. He mistakes Hannay's efforts to keep Margaret quiet about the newspaper for a romantic intrigue. At a certain level it is. The tracking shot (23c) that is the reverse of his entrance (11b) depicts the husband leaving the table. Its dissymmetry records the difference in the situations he has entered and left. Though the camera moves with him, the background figures at the table are now out of focus (whereas in the entering shot *he* was out of focus), and he occupies a middle zone in the frame. It describes the emotional meaning of the scene from his point of view. It is the depiction from a distance of his confusion. The camera movement is motivated by the pace of his walk, though outside the house, just at the end of the tracking shot, the camera asserts its own power, and after he has stopped, continues to move slightly further to the right (24c, d). Our view, this movement signifies, is not identified completely with his. When the attitudes of the young couple are openly conspiratorial (26), the suppression of any sound, though there is an evident source in the image, only reinforces, from the husband's point of view, the fact that he is excluded, literally outside. Formally, it shows that the true sense of the scene is withheld from him. Because we are looking over his shoulder, and his face is turned away (24c, d), the spectator has little reliable sense of what the Crofter is feeling, though we are supposed to speculate. This relation of sound and image defines a structure of misperception in which silence becomes an empty sign that invites the audience to fill in the husband's response. Given a more informed frame of reference, the spectator interprets the enigma of what seems to be said in a quite different way from the husband, who sees in the surface evidence what he already imagines, or projects. The husband's exit from the house implicates him in the action in a way that suggests his view has gone from suspicion to masochistic voyeurism. The shots from the inside of the house (25, 27) do show his face and provide the spectator evidence to confirm what we only imagined and projected on him. The fade-out to blackness gives his view a further and final significance, portending a dark and ominous future.

The general strategy for depicting the husband's glance is objectification. Typically, in shots that we are asked to read as the husband's "point of view," he is physically present in the frame. This presence is doubled by his literal appearance and by the movement of the camera that establishes a kinesthetic correspondence between our movement and his. At the same time we are given a privileged position behind him: we see him and also what he sees along the same axis. We are necessarily distanced. In the concluding shots (24d, 26), the framing is doubled: there is the actual shot frame and a set of inner frames structured by the window. Thus what he sees becomes a framed image. An analogy is implied between the husband and the spectator. While the Crofter's viewing fully engages us, the effect of the visual doublings and distancings is to present and describe, but also to qualify our sense of identification with his view. Though a basic constitutent of the rhetorical structure of the sequence, his viewing is depicted as a systematic misreading of their collusion. The literal distance between the camera and himself corresponds figuratively to the implied narrator's critique and commentary on the interests that motivate that viewing. The narrator makes the Crofter's view an object of interpretation. By this structure, the spectator both knows the husband's state of mind and fears for the safety of the characters, with whom we sympathize, but who are not aware they are being watched.

The implied narrator is present in the text through the way he narrates the story. Rhetoric, in other words, defines the formal structure of the act of making and reading meaning. The signs of the narrator's authority are the concrete structures that exhibit the "story" to the spectator. Chapter 1 revealed the connection of these ideas by showing that a text establishes by a power of organization, we called the agency of the narrator, a point of view different from any character or ideal spectator. In this chapter, I suggest that the difference between the meaning of the events for the characters and for the implied spectator in both *Stagecoach* and *The 39 Steps* is evidence that the distinction between story and representation is a matter of making and remaking, or interpreting, meaning, and that it is a sign of a mode of action specific to the implied narrator. This sequence provides grounds for considering the signifying structure of surrogation and the production of meaning through point of view.

Rhetoric integrates story and representation by organizing a vantage point on the action of character. In *The 39 Steps* the narrator allies and distinguishes the spectator's view from the characters', and defines the events in specular terms as recognition, exposure, and misperception. Surrogation is a strategy that structures a certain form of address to the spectator. The figure who assumes this responsibility in a film is not usually a narrator-persona, but a character fully involved in the action. Surrogation functions by seeming, in some fashion, to ascribe the authority for the imagery to the depicted character or to a functional center that makes a sequence of disjunct shots legible to a spectator. Reading makes sense of the organization of the fictional space of the story in terms of views on the action of character. The meaning for the spectator is mediated through the meaning the event is shown to have for the central character. The difference between the two orders of meaning, between character and spectator, and the structures that enact it, constitute the signifying structure of surrogation.

The possibility of disjunction, suspension, anticipation or return to a functioning "center," demonstrates the narrator's independence and defines his role in the nature of making meaning. Insofar as the set-up in (4a) anticipates the new location of the center before it is established and before its meaning to Hannay is evident, it is a sign of the narrator's (momentary) independence of character and of his own freedom of movement. The shot locates the center definitively only by Hannay's sitting down. The continuity effected by the center is not fixed, but can be interrupted, restored, relocated or exchanged. The moment when the husband enters the house (10), an unexpected interruption of the center's location constitutes and is experienced as shock. When the husband passes across the frame, eclipsing Hannay, the break is reconstituted, retroactively, as exchange. Even if momentarily, the center can be open, or, like a linguistic shifter, occupied from moment to moment by differing inhabitants, its function of legibility is preserved. Its logic is altogether impersonal. As a structure that accommodates surrogation, centering is basic to the spectator's reading of specific meaning effects. On a formal level, reading requires the spectator to occupy the figurative position of the character who defines the center and to appreciate the significance of the imagery seen from that position. In this sequence from *The 39 Steps*, centering creates an identification with Hannay, and then by its rupture and dis-location introduces a new perceptual system, the husband's, to substitute for and contest the first. The impersonality of the exchange suggests that the narrator's representation depends on images of the body or the view of a character, but that he is never limited to only representing, nor to authorizing, such views. Insofar as the view seen from the center is both meaningful and criticized, the Crofter's misperception is emblematic of the relations of analogy and independence that define the manner of integration of the two levels of discourse. The meaning-of-the-text, insofar as it is a view, is made by a specific kind of depiction: a showing.

The sequence as a whole is the exposition of a situation, but the view it ascribes to the husband, suspicion, amounts to characterization. The sense of suspicion being enacted before our eyes—he is in the frame, but we see their response—is precisely structured by a sequence of certain images to signify his interiority. The cut between (10b) and (11a) (before the Crofter appears in the frame) makes an assertion by formal means: this is his view of them.

The cut functions as a predicting sign to relate the seeing subject and the object seen. The narrator states the relation between the persons in the two shots: the organization of the image shows us the limitations of his view by its depiction. The starts and stops of the tracking shot put his error before us and characterize it as misinterpretation. The structure of the difference between meaning-for-character and meaning-for-spectator is in the way it is disclosed. Disclosure of the error corresponds to the Crofter's passage from the frame: it shows that though we share his field of view, his is a false view. This is the structure of the spectator's recognition. The narrator's relation to the views of character is one of temporary appropriation.

The dissociation of view from narrator's viewpoint in this passage underlines that distinction as it is related to signification and to belief. The sequence shows that questioning a view is accomplished by another view and that the spectator's conviction in a view is not simply a product of a syntactical logic. Reading, as producing the meaning of the text, is related to the emotional investment or criticism made by the spectator. The aspect of the response, articulated as the difference between the meaning of the event to character and to spectator, might be called *force*. It is a feature of signification elicited and structured by the film, and is specific to the narrator's point of view on the story. It describes the requirement of the spectator's committing himself to imaginatively occupying that depicted fictional role, to feeling the character from the inside, but also to recognizing, by the way that view is located in the moral structure of the text, the difference of his position from ours. When the force of the text is in effect, the spectator perceives an identity with a character not by any extraneous or undisciplined projection, but because that identification is specifically structured by the film. It locates, by the process of participation and reading, the relation between a character's views and the point of view authorized by the film.

The action of the moving camera might serve to clarify the position of the implied narration in the structure of surrogation, and to define further the relation between representation and story. It is evidence that the narrator-in-the-text is a moving, embodied persona whose function is exhibition and interpretation. Movement of the camera in this shot (1a, b, c) is in two phases. After a dissolve, the camera "follows" Hannay's walk away from us by a movement in the same direction that begins after Hannay has stopped and taken his place by the door. It continues forward, and then as he turns his head toward Margaret and the Crofter, stops for a few moments in the scale shown in (1b). In the second phase, just when the husband exits the frame, the camera resumes its forward motion and stops for the final time with the wife's question, "Will you not come in?" Are all the stops and starts "motivated" in the same way by the action? What is the relation of camera movement to Hannay? The first start appears to recreate the route of Hannay's walk toward the couple, but because Hannay is already at the threshold when the camera starts its movement, its motion does not actually depict the correspondence of the movements. The second start is quite different. Coming after a stop, it is read as an initiation of movement. Whereas the motivation for the first start is Hannay's completion of an action, the second movement forward coincides with the husband's exit. After the husband's exit, the first stop seems retrospectively to signify a respect for or response to an implied prohibition against moving closer. The camera (second) motion forward explicitly imitates Hannay's, and seems to suggest a psychological explanation. The first stop coincides with Hannay's turning his head toward the couple. The second stop, in contrast to any other camera movements, is not explicitly keyed to the action in the frame. Its primary determination is not related to the action within the frame, but to the value of scale as an element of pictorial composition. In this way, camera movement and graphic scale can be regarded as correlative features of signification. Movement, rather than framing as such, seems to control the force of our reading.

One interpretation of the relation of camera movements to the action is that they are to be described as an analogy or as a response to the psychological situation of the central character. Thus the movement of the camera would correspond to Hannay's sense of approach, to the respectful distance proper to such a meeting, and finally to a feeling of growing intimacy. This kind of interpretation does not explain, though, relevant features of the camera movement. Why does the camera not begin to move until Hannay stops? Why does the camera stop where it does the last time? As a theoretical rationale, what legitimates the sense that the camera's "motivation" is anything more than a consequence of an effect of simple sequence and succession? What justifies a psychological or an analogical inference?

There is another explanation. What the specifics of the camera motion give evidence for is not that an analogy exists between the camera and the psychological state presumed to exist already in the character—an analogy that makes the camera motion an imitative response—rather, the details of the movement are evidence that the action of the camera itself, with motions so much like those of the human body in action, creates an interpretation. These "actions" of the camera are read as those of a fully embodied narrator. The force of the camera movement creates in us an identification with the narrator that is transferred, as a schema of interpretation, onto the action of characters shown within the frame. It determines their meaning and allows them to be read (back) as having a certain "analogous" sense. The narrator interprets the significance of the physical movements that constitute the depicted action by the mobile power of representation that creates, delimits and defines his gesture for the spectator. The forward movement has the expository function of introducing the characters into a symbolic or at least significant composition in a scale appropriate to their number and to our need to read their faces and gestures. Whatever analogy the camera movement proposes, an aspect of its movement as I have suggested here, will acknowledge that the action it depicts is being presented for a spectator and is not simply to be accounted for on the characters' terms. Though the camera's emphatic forward movement asks the audience to (mis) understand its function as (simply) the instrument for the exposition of a better view of what is already there, by its stops and starts, it brings meaning into effect.

The result of the camera's movement is not just the exhibition of the scene. Inseparably, though less obviously, it enacts an interpretation of the depicted action by structures of force that call for spectator identification. It is a feature of a rhetoric that asks to be seen not as the creation and figuration of meaning, but as its simple display.

How is rhetorical organization of the narrative in this sequence from *The 39 Steps* related to the spectator's viewing? The film puts the surrogate before the audience so that his views of objects have, at a certain level, their own integrity and independence, and are understood to define his interests and his character. In turn these views are seen from an independent and outside position by an ordering agency, that while having complex relations of alliance to the views of character, subordinates them to the narrative exposition. The relation between character and narrator in this text is not, in other words, that of a dialogue between equal parts. Rather the narrator plots the confrontation of the depicted "characters." Whatever their independence or filiation, in the last instance, they take their place in a hierarchy ordered by the authority-in-the-text. That is, the views of characters are located by the narrative point of view. As the depiction of the Crofter's view suggests, the scope of representation extends to interpreting and exhibiting meaning made at another level of the discourse, the story. Reading and its effects are related to the interests of character in the way the text modulates and interprets the force of that position. The example of the moving camera, both in (1) and (11) is a case in point. The anxiety and frustration felt for Hannay as he attempts to see the paper (4a) does not completely give way to the shock and surprise of the husband's entrance (11). Rather these feelings tend to coexist. Such a dynamic of reading as a response to the text negotiates multiple appeals and contexts that might be summarized as the modalities of temporality (initiation, suspension, interrruption, retrospection, conclusion, etc.) and versions of personalization (identification, distancing, exchange).

How does the narrative serve as a support for meaningful structures of the text that are not themselves part of the action? If we consider again the discovery of the newspaper, we remember that the paper and its movements provided the pretext or occasion for characterizing certain important acts of perception. The most dramatic "events" of the text, those that advanced the plot and explained its movement, had to do with forms of seeing. At one moment in the story, Hannay's long-delayed reading of the newspaper headlines is represented in a way not fully located in or justified by the depicted action. This moment is framed by strictly narrative shots which show Hannay picking up the paper and then putting it down (11c, 15a). The three shots within this framing structure however, in particular the lighting of the lamp (13), are only loosely connected or justified by the action of any narrative agency. The Crofter's reaching into his pocket for a match is barely detectable—the relation between the action and the actor is suppressed. The result is that the lighting of the lamp is not specifically located in the space of action. Likewise, the sound produced by the striking of the match (12), the only sound associated with these shots, does not have an evident source in the image. It functions as an announcement of a significant moment. The light gradually dispels the darkness and illuminates the page, disclosing a headline that if seen by the others would expose Hannay's identity as mechanic (for another false identity, murderer). As a representation it is constituted by silence, hyperbolic scale, the lighting itself, and an exemption from an explicit spatial definition. It is a figuratively heightened description of the meaning of Hannay's reading, and of the recognition of his precarious position.

A short time later there is a more explicitly figurative shot. It shows Hannay with Margaret caught both by the light of the husband's candle, and arrested by the police searchlight that penetrates the window that is *now covered with bars*.

The house in which Hannay has taken shelter has by this trope become a prison. Hannay's guilt and innocence, the terms in which the story of the newspaper is articulated, makes the presence of light explicitly a sign of apprehension and of imprisonment. The shot from outside the house through the barred window is not exactly a representation of Hannay's apprehension of his being trapped either from his point of view or from that of his would-be captors, but by someone moveable in space, yet figuratively close to Hannay's sense of apprehension, who interprets the meaning of the event by symbolization: the narrator is Nobody.

As a figurative icon of danger, whose spatiality in this respect is outside the narrative, it takes its place in a system of metaphorical connotations, closely connected to the terms of the narrative, that define what we could call a *theme*. Hannay is exposed by the light of the husband's candle (falsely?) as seducer, and by the searchlight, as murderer. His guise as mechanic has been exposed. In this precarious situation where the truth of his identity is doubted by nearly everyone, and where the agents of exposure are both mistaken, it is only the shadows and recesses of the house, the darkness of the night, and Margaret's gift of the dark-colored raincoat, that can hide and shelter Hannay from wrongful imprisonment. The system of connotation locates thematically the tones of black and white of the actual image, the significance of shadow and light that convey the mood, the figurative effect of the lighting of the lamp and the darkening prospect of liberty signified by the bars. As an image complex they collectively take on significance by reference to the premises of the narrative and in that way to the structure of views organized in terms of Hannay's guilt or innocence. As a system, the values, light and dark, define an ironic, nearly paranoiac inversion of their standard meaning. Detached, like locale, from the strictly necessary require- ments of the story, connotation stands outside the "narrative object." As a system of signs it comments, with an authority whose source is undeter- mined, on the meaning of the action. It is like the scene of the action, but it takes its general significance, by analogy, from the central character. However much it relates to the narrative, connotation functions to give the text a sense beyond the meaning of the events of the story or the depiction of character. It interprets the narrative in the direction of theme.

This thematic meaning stands in a complex relation both to our study of stills and to our "natural" viewing of the film. There is the sense that we do not have to interpret the action, and that the study of the stills promotes certain aspects of the text to an importance they do not seem to carry in a natural viewing. The full speed reading produces responses that are not a consideration of the weighty issues of guilt and innocence as such, but excitement, suspense, etc. Rather, these terms, guilt and innocence, seem to define a situation or pretext, not its elaboration as a theme. But these terms are explicitly and significantly related to an account of the rhetoric, to the rationale for the structure of views, studied through these stills. Perhaps this difference can be attributed to the effects of reading. The text makes the occasion an object of spectator interest, the newspaper and its "adventures," only a pretext, and largely insignificant, after its discovery. Its movements, I have shown, are secondary to characters' perceptions. Is the mechanism of the advance of the narrative, like the newspaper, explicitly treated by the text as worthless? Does the newspaper function in this structure as the McGuffin? The paper's function might be regarded as emblematic of the relation within the text of narrative to meaning: in its forward motion the film disposes of its narrative object by a kind of cannibalization that produces meaning effects. The narrative agency transforms the story into a second (characterization) and third (thematic) system of sense. Reading would be the consumption of the narrative object to produce systems of readable, that is recognizable, meaning that simultaneously articulate one order of significance and suppress another "lower" level of knowledge of the film (i.e. the structures of continuity, change of viewpoint, etc.). The natural reading, by its distracting speed and by the conditions it induces in the audience—of shock, suspense, identification, anxiety, anticipation and fading—requires strategies that tend to block the leisurely search for the meaning of the image and the relation between images as if they were taken as a set of stills. It is the motion of the action and its movement of disclosure that so fascinates the spectator and encourages the production of effects that foreclose a conscious reconstruction of their strategy. The temporality of the narration, in part, inflects the affect, the force of spectator involvement. A set of stills is a way, then, of recovering the meaningful structure suppressed by the natural speed of exhibition. Because it provides the time for a reflective, atemporal reconstruction of strategies, of meaning, the analysis of stills carries with it a certain bias.

The stills that accompany this essay are both "text" and evidence. Their selection no doubt was an act of interpretation. They economically record and preserve significant features of camera movement and action within the frame. They make it possible to begin to account for those structures that might escape attention in a natural viewing in a rigorous and systematic way. Arranging them on a sequence of pages seemed like a useful way of preserving a record of those relations at a glance.

Though both the object of study and an interpretation, the stills do constitute a kind of "text" that makes reference to and attempts to preserve the signifying structure of the original experience. They were not chosen to illustrate a concept, but as a text. The guiding theoretical notions of this chapter, authority, point of view, connotation, and the account of the relation between representation and story emerge from the problem of accounting for the concrete relations among these stills and of our experience of the film. These concepts have an empirical standing by the way they are related to the structures of the narrative.

The stills are cited and referred to in the text of the chapter as objects of analysis and as evidence of the mode of film's narration and of the place and function of the authority-in-the-text. They are used to generate and establish the terms of a certain account of problems of filmic meaning and to explain the functioning of structures specific to the sequence. The hermeneutic circle may seem to be closed by this relation of stills and essay. The stills are included here, though, to provide the reader with the grounds for a critical assessment of the method and to consider the standing of the theoretical results.

An account of filmic narration, or of its authority, cannot ignore the spectator's experience of the temporality or the natural movement of the film. "Reading," as the apprehension of a semblance of life in the film, I have suggested, is specifically linked to the force of our identification with character. This aspect of signification, the spectator's progressive involvement in the action, that accounts for his response, depends on the natural speed of unfolding in the darkened projection hall. Stills do not represent that aspect of the text. For that dimension, it is necessary to return to or to recall the experience.

That stills do not adequately represent the aspects of camera motion bears on both the description of the spectator's experience of the film, and on the formulation of the function of authority-in-the-text. The first shot of the sequence, for example, as I have pointed out above, is a dolly forward. It is represented by three stills (1a, b, c) that correspond to the indicated points in the dialogue. This notation does not show, though, whether the camera moves forward evenly, or whether it stops, and then starts again, or what its relation is to action in the frame. These stills have many advantages, but are incomplete for an analysis of the operation of narrator-in-the-text considered as the power of free movement. The narrator's invisibility here, in the form of stilled motion, is a sign of his agency.

The narrator's power of exhibition is expressed literally in the movement of the camera. In the way it constitutes and interprets the field of view, the moving camera acts both as a form of narrative exposition and as the figuration of the implied narrator as he moves from place to place in the unwinding of the film. Though idealized and structured to persuade the spectator to think of the action of the body of the character and not that of the implied narrator, the camera's action asks to be read as intentional human action. Whereas shot/counter shot seems to deny the embodiment of the narrator (only the cut is the sign of his intervening presence), in the case of the moving camera, his power of exhibition is represented literally as movement. The images of the film are to be accounted for not just on the model of the eye, but also for reference to the imaginative action of bodies in space. The text, in its imaginative organization, materializes the bodily image of authority. We might say that the narrator-in-the-text establishes his credibility by demonstrating his power to establish, to present, and to move coherently from place to place.

Narration in this text consists of the exhibition of the story and a commentary on it. This delimits the scope of the narrator's symbolic action: the power to make an interpretation and to put us in a position to see it as a theme. He interprets events through a succession of views *of* and views *on* characters and through the articulation of a point of view. His judgment is implied by, and is inseparable from, the appropriation and critique of views of characters. In this sense his point of view arbitrates and locates the views of others.

In this kind of sequence, film's mode of narration is like the indirect narration of the novel. Meaning is mediated by an implied narrator whose report is realized by views of and on the character. The medium of significance though, direct forms of presentation of gesture and word transmitted by the image, is like drama. The change of vantage point under the control of the narrator presents and interprets the actions and defines this mode of filmic narration.

The filmic narrator is not on the same level of action as the character; that is to say, depicted as a narrator. Rather, like drama, the film depicts characters which, as physical figures shown by the image, all have the same degree of reality. The film organizes a set of views that could not be accounted for by any character's view of himself. This is to say that film insists in its narratological structure, if not in its effect, on the difference between narrator and character. This distinction between the two levels of discourse describes the organization of this difference. As a signifying structure, surrogation establishes both relations of analogy and independence between the implied narrator and character. The structures of disjunction, anticipation, movement, distance, and critique that determine the differences are evidence of and define the scope of the narrator's independence, and of his power to locate us with respect to the action. The relation between the two levels, narrator/spectator and character, describes an economy of shift, transit, exchange and circulation of fictional locations. Continuity of action and the maintenance of center are signs of the formal impersonality of this structure. As an ensemble of strategies, this rhetoric tells the story, locates the characters' views, and within this set of narratological structures, articulates a point of view on that story.

The place of the implied narrator, like that of the spectator, is ambiguous between person and place. He is not depicted as such in the space of the characters, though there are evident signs of his action: most obviously, an intelligible sequence of images. He is present rather by signs of his absence. His invisibility, ubiquity, impersonality, multipersonality, and the traces of his movement, define his action within the text as the maker and exhibitor of meaning. The narrator is associated with the exhibition of images but is, ambiguously, both *in* and *behind* them. He takes a position in and on the story. Considered in this way, narration is not an act of invention but of exhibition and interpretation. Narration, not narrative, is the province of authority.

Appendix B

Stills and Dialogue from
The 39 Steps

Dissolve in.
CROFTER. Here's a gentleman. (a) He'll stay with us till tomorrow morning.

1a

HANNAY. Your daughter?
CROFTER. My wife. (b)

1b

MARGARET. Will you not come in? (c)

1c

MARGARET. Here's your bed. . .These will have to be cleaned. Could you sleep there do you think?

2

MARGARET. You'll be tired.
HANNAY. I'll say I am. I'm on the trail
looking for a job.
MARGARET. Won't you sit down please
while I go on with our supper.
HANNAY. Thank you.

3

4a

4b

5

6a

6b

HANNAY. Been in these parts long? (c)
MARGARET. No. I'm from Glasgow. Did
you ever see it?
HANNAY. (off) No.
MARGARET. Oh you should see Hal Street
with all its fine shops. And Algia Street on
Saturday night. With the names and the
lights. And the cinema, concert, and
crowds. It's Saturday night tonight.

6c

HANNAY. You certainly don't get those
things out here. (d)
MARGARET. No.

6d

HANNAY. (off) You miss them? (a)
MARGARET. Sometimes.

7a

HANNAY. (off) Well I haven't been to
Glasgow, (b) but I've been to Edinburgh
and Montreal and London. I'll tell you all
about London at supper. (c)

7b

7c

MARGARET. John wouldn't approve of
that I doubt.
HANNAY. Why not? (d)
MARGARET. (off) He says its best not. . .

7d

MARGARET. . . . to think of such places. . .

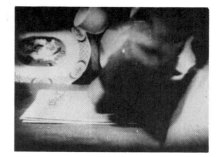

8

MARGARET. (off) . . .and all the wickedness.
HANNAY. What do you want to know?(a)

9a

MARGARET. Well, is it true that all the
ladies paint their toenails?
HANNAY. Some of them do.
MARGARET. Do London ladies look beau-
tiful?
HANNAY. They do. . . (b)

9b

HANNAY. (off) . . .(a) but they wouldn't if
you were beside them.

10a

MARGARET. (off) You ought not to say that. (b)
CROFTER. What ought. . .

10b

CROFTER. (off). . .he not to say? (a)

11a

HANNAY. I was just saying to your wife that I prefer living in town than living in the country. (b)

11b

CROFTER. (off) God made the country. (on) Is the supper ready yet woman?
HANNAY. Do you mind if I have a look at your paper?
CROFTER. Oh, I don't mind. (c)

11c

(off) Sound of match being struck.

12

13

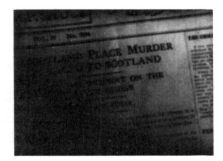

14a

14b

CROFTER. You didn't tell me your name.
HANNAY. Hammond.
CROFTER. Well Mr. Hammond, if you put
down that paper, I'll say a blessing.
HANNAY. (a) Yes, surely. (b)

15a

15b

CROFTER. Sanctify these bounteous mer-
cies to us miserable sinners. . .

16

CROFTER. (off). . .Oh Lord make us truly
thankful. . .

17

CROFTER. (off). . .for them and for all thy manifold blessings. . .

18

CROFTER. (off). . .and continually turn our hearts. . .

19

CROFTER. (off). . .from wickedness. . .

20a

20b

CROFTER. (off). . .and from wordly things. . .

21

CROFTER. (on). . .unto thee. . .

22

CROFTER. (on). . .Amen. (a) I forgot to lock the barn. (b)

23a

23b

23c

No sound accompanies 24,25,26,27

24a

24b

24c

24d

25

26

Fade out.

27

3

Narration as Interpretation:
The Rhetoric of *Au Hasard, Balthazar*

The study of the structure of filmic narration, the act of showing events to a spectator, is different from the study of the narrative itself. In particular, an explanation of narration and of the organization of narrative space calls for a study of how the text mediates the functions of narrator, character, and spectator. Generally, what is at issue in an analysis of the structure of filmic narration, at one level, is the function and power of the agency, or the subject, that enunciates the narrative, that presents the discourse. In this matter, Oudart's analysis has a specific advantage over the traditional account. It invokes a mechanism in which what the spectator sees is mediated by the view of an off-screen character. The shot/reverse shot "system of the suture" is then taken as the paradigm for the construction of narrative space. But an explanation or a theory whose principal logic is ascription—referring an account of a shot to the authority, to the glance of a depicted character—can neither explain third-person shots adequately, nor assimilate them to first-person shots, nor provide a basis for a coherent account of the logic of shots of either kind. Though the system of the suture invokes a subject of *enunciation*, the off-screen character, it is only an apparent one, and exists on the same narrative level as the depicted character, that of the fiction (*enonce*). Thus the system does not offer adequate terms—ones that comprehend the level of the narration proper (*enunciation*)—to account for the production of the character whose glance subtends the space.

The "narrator," we may suppose, exhibits the images of the film and by control of camera position, *mise-en-scène*, editing, and sound, positions the spectator in a certain relation to the depicted world. He constructs too, through the use of the character as a medium of communication, views on the world of the story. While the character's views have their own integrity, it is the place of the narrator to exhibit them as views, and to make us see them as part of a larger picture through the power of his commentary. That is, the narrator is related to characters by both structures of analogy (he can appropriate their gaze) and independence (he can show their views as simply views). This is the basis of the distinction between the two orders of significant structure: *representation* (the set of rhetorical mechanisms through which the narrator presents the story to the spectator), and *story* (the actions, speech, and perceptions of the character, whose glance is like other actions: an "object" to be depicted).

Narration as a communicational act is a process of interpreting the significance of a character's experience through exhibiting it cinematically for the spectator. As such it is part of narrative theory to examine and explain the linkages between different orders of seeing integrated within a film: "shot," "point of view shot," "character's point of view," and "narrative point of view." The narration exhibits the action and produces an interpretation of it by coordinating these various levels of seeing: it makes and discloses "narrative point of view" by positioning the "spectator-in-the-text." The articulation of critical or interpretive judgment, by the control of narrative point of view, marks the intervention of the power specific to the narrator.

An explanation of the production and significance of narrative space cannot be limited to that tendered by any "ideal spectator," or of the structuring function of a character's glance or "point of view." What is necessary for an account of the production of fictional space and the inscription of the spectator in it is the same as for an account of the structure of narration: a model of the productive mediations among narrator/character/spectator. Whether or not it is necessary to assume that the investment of authority in the camera's framing represents a conventionally analyzable human act, narrative agency is a function necessary for an analysis of the production of textual effects.

This essay on Bresson's *Au Hasard, Balthazar* is part of a continuing study of the relation between the narrator's act of relating the character's story and the spectator's act of reading it. This particular film is of special interest to the study of narration and of point of view (both character's and narrator's) because its central and unifying figure is nonhuman: the donkey Balthazar. The choice of Balthazar as the subject of the story (it is framed by his birth and death) creates effects integral to the significance of the work but imposes on the narration certain special problems. In a conventional narrative, for example, a central character whose "consciousness" is constructed and appropriated by the film generally functions to mediate the world of the film to the spectator. Thus the cuts within a point-of-view sequence are formal markers of the significant action of this character, the direction of his or her attention. A conventional rhetoric allows the spectator to infer characters' "views" from shots. Filmic narration works so that this kind of inference constructs "character." In *Au Hasard, Balthazar*, however, the central depicted consciousness is not human, nor is it anthropomorphized exactly, and it does not function as transparent medium. Likewise, the human characters in the film, whose fortunes are paralleled with Balthazar, are opaque. What follows, then, is a study of the aims and strategies of narration in a text whose rhetorical form is articulated on special premises.

Bresson's *Au Hasard, Balthazar* is a text which makes use of the signifying structure of medieval allegory for the announcement of its doctrine. But at the same time it renders ineffectual an attending result of that structure—the audience's identification with the work as an illustration, example, or object of imitation. The film-text undertakes to testify to a religious truth: that there is a divinity behind the chance events of life and the suffering of man. The problem of the text is its authentication of this claim. It refuses an appeal to ecclesiastical authority, and founds its claim to authenticity and belief on the spectator's experience of the film. Though its basic strategy is allegory, the film does not wish to lose its claim to truth to life by appearing too explicitly as an illustration or demonstration of an abstract or bookish system. It makes its appeal to truth neither by asking to be considered in a religious tradition nor by attempting to certify an historical event (though it does document the personal history of the donkey Balthazar from birth to death). It undertakes to validate its religious claims by the spectator's apprehension of the "realness" of the depicted world: the three-dimensional volume of the space of the action and the corporality of its persons. The text wishes, in other words, to establish a religious truth incarnated in the events of the story, events which appear irrational in their (secular) justice and disordered by chance.

Such requirements make the central problem of the film the way it establishes and orders the relations between literal and figurative meanings of its depicted events. This difference of level corresponds to the meaning that events have in the "story" for characters and their meaning on the level of "representation." The figure of Balthazar—his meaning(s) for the characters and for us—is perhaps the best example of this difference of interpretations. The first level, through an ensemble of mediating structures that tie the representation to the story, supports and announces the second, the implied, not openly stated, meaning, which as a theological significance, returns to transform and reorganize the first.

Au Hasard, Balthazar does not though attempt to instruct the audience, nor even to encourage the emulation of its central figure. The life of this saint is not held up for imitation. Indeed the film seeks to inhibit pity or identification that in Christian aesthetics is normally associated with moral or exemplary identification. We see Balthazar and the characters with whom he is explicitly compared suffer, but his suffering is neither to be admired nor emulated, and our usual expectation of a figure of this kind, and what we extend to him, our pity, is systematically shown by the film to be inappropriate. The retardation of our tendency to identification with character, a retardation of feeling that the rhetoric of the film accomplishes by a coherent ensemble of strategies for depicting character, is in the service of another end. These events are meant to be contemplated as a religious image of man's unredeemed suffering. The film locates the nature or cause of this suffering beyond the categories of psychological or moral experience. In the depiction of such a world, in which the forces of cruelty and domination are joined in violent and merciless combat with good, responses like pity or moral condemnation are shown to be inappropriate. The film's denial of our feelings of identification with the suffering figures of the story is transformed by mediating features of the representation to an experience that restores to the depicted person the mystery and depth of interiority best understood, the film asserts, in theological categories. Through the spectator's experience, the film gives a second meaning to the spectacle of passion, love, humiliation and cruelty he has witnessed, a meaning that points toward or implies an allegorical level. It testifies to what Bresson has set out from the first to demonstrate, the full and irreducible mystery of Balthazar's story, and to the unseen and mysterious power beyond naming that stands behind man's suffering in this world.

It is in this context that the specific problem of the narration of *Au Hasard, Balthazar* emerges in its full implications. How does a film that takes a donkey as its central "character" make sense, and make the sense it does? The narratives studied in the first two chapters, I showed in detail, were organized by the depiction of a figure whose consciousness, whose being as a character, mediated our perception of events. This chapter considers the organization of a text framed by Balthazar's birth and death that tells his story. In this way the continuing set of problems posed by the thesis—the relation between representation and story, the construction of the narrator's point of view and its relation to character, and the description of place of the spectator and the nature of his reading—can be considered in a text whose unconventional functioning invites, and whose understanding or appreciation could profit from, just such an inquiry. On the basis, then, of a sequence presented by the coordination of stills, sound and dialogue, I intend to show that making sense of such a subject is achieved by a coherent ensemble of signifying and rhetorical strategies that defines a particular form of narrative and textual organization. By analyzing Balthazar's mode of being, and Arnold, a human character whose fortunes are parallel and intertwined with the donkey's, I expect a delineation of a rhetoric articulated on premises and aims different from films we have (provisionally) called "classical." I expect too, a further, theoretical, clarification of the relation between levels of "representation" and "story" in film texts.

The sequence showing Arnold's "celebration" and death raises the problem of depicting a form of life of one who, though called by his enemies a "half wit," can also be seen as a paradigmatically Bressonian character. It raises the matter of the commentary in the film in a way tied explicitly to the problem of locating Balthazar's formal and thematic significance and of describing the functioning of the allegory. What is significant about Arnold and what raises the question of describing a sequence organized around his presence, can be seen in shots (22–35) and (51–63). Consider his relation to Girard. It is developed by four pairs of shot/counter shot in which both characters occupy the frame, one nearly frontal, the other from the back. The angle on Girard is uniformly symmetrical to the one on Arnold, constituting a symmetry of framing inconsistent with Girard's evident domination that amounts to assault. Arnold passively accepts Girard's insults and obeys his orders. The two look at each other in a way that shows at the same time who they are to themselves and to the other. The film establishes a specific connection between Girard's assault on Arnold and the breaking of the mirror through a repetition of the remarkable shot, from a set-up behind Arnold's back, of Girard's hand reaching first for a glass, then for a bottle. Girard's reaching for the bottle (29b) comes after Arnold gives back a blank stare as an answer to Girard's order to drink and is, evidently, a substitution or last resort for Girard's not having been able to bring Arnold to a sufficiently submissive destruction. For Girard, Arnold's blank stare is emblematic of a presence (concentrated in a look) that like the literal mirror, holds up an intolerable image of his person before his own conscience. What Girard sees in Arnold at this moment and what so calls for his destruction, or its displacement as breaking up the cafe, is the truth and reproach that evil apprehends in its self regard. What Girard wishes to destroy is the fact, and its inescapability, of Arnold's unblinking gaze. And Arnold unblinkingly sees or recognizes in Girard something equally profound: his torment from the beginning of time, a fate against which appeal is pointless, nothing, his destiny, his death. That embracing this recognition is the meaning of his look is confirmed by the way he participates fully, that is passively, in the ritual of passage that Girard has prepared: the kisses, the assent to the long journey, the departure on the back of Balthazar. The symmetry and framing signify their roles as dialectical combatants. Framing does not relate to a psychology of power or to the domination that the one enforces over the other, but establishes and defines the interlocked nature of their destiny of condition. Arnold knows perhaps better than anyone in the film that for whatever reasons, with inexorable precision, evil accomplishes its ends. It is in this sense that the drama is to be imagined in theological terms.

The theological coordinates of the action of these beings are active and passive. Girard approaches and addresses Arnold, motivates the movement of the camera in (25), (29), (30), (31) by reaching with his hand, throwing, leaping on the bar, and actively initiating the destruction of the cafe. Having seen what he does in (30) and (31), Girard's hands and feet accomplishing the actions, the spectator takes the subsequent images of pure destruction (33c, 34, 35) as the consequence of his off-screen (implied) agency. Arnold on the other hand is unresponsive and still. Through the scene, his face shows the same resigned, nearly blank, expression, the sign of an unchanging condition. Thus it is that Arnold's back is as expressive of his theological position in the depicted world as his front. It also establishes his corporality. Bresson cuts from Girard to Arnold to show us the absence, infuriating for Girard, of any change. His position in the sequence is summarized in the "reaction shot" (32) to the crashing of the broken glass: he sits staring blankly, his hands folded inward on his knees, jostled slightly by the dancers.

Arnold's condition of being acted upon, as with Girard's approach, is associated with our seeing the action from behind his back. From that position we are aware as soon as the confrontation begins, of Arnold's height, or rather his being "above," particularly in a sequence with such precise formal symmetries. He is clearly distinguished in each shot from Girard and from the crowd by framing that reminds us of his fact. It is a position of elevation that seems to make him vulnerable to Arnold, and curiously, outside the perception of the others. From Balthazar's descent from grazing with the sheep high in the mountains, as a foal, to his ascent and death amidst the sheep at the end, the typology of space, even in the organization of relations in this moment, corresponds to the mysterious symbolism of election. Arnold's height and stillness are contrasted to the activity, the movement, of the agency of evil.

Arnold does not share in the celebration, typified by the movement of the music. All around, with him, still, at the center, are people dancing. With both the lawyer (4) and with Girard, Arnold is located in a middle zone, of stillness, set off from the foreground and background by the bopping, anglar rhythmic movements that surround him. While out of focus, the action in the nearest and furthest zones defines the spatiality of the image as one of full scenic volume. That is, our object of interest in shots of medium scale is explicitly located at a plane in space that is seen as a depth. The foreground, as a plane of significant action, is restricted to a setting off and to an unveiling of the principal action. Movement in the foreground frequently masks, and then, as the dancing figures move away, discloses what is significant—Arnold. The turning of a head as in (4a, b) or Girard's coming forward, head down (23a, b), accomplishes a similar end: establishing and commenting on a relation between the principal figure and the scene. The structure and effect of masking and revealing, within the mise-en-scène of the single image, establishes the different relation the spectator has with

Arnold and with the scene. Arnold, as a character, is not revealed as the action is by the structures that unveil him to our view. Even when we know nothing of his interiority, indeed because of that, he is not shown in the process of being revealed, but as revealed. It is this continuous condition that accounts in part for the expressiveness of his stillness and back, and of his impassive eye and physiognomy. In contrast, Girard's actions do properly "disclose" him. The découpage of the scene responds to this difference.

What is so horrifying about the destruction in this scene is not just its violence or its calculation, but that it is not opposed, that it continues. Our sympathies in the matter are complex. From the beginning we are aware that it is Arnold who will pay. The crashing of glass, though, is a matter of as much indifference to him as the bopping music played on the jukebox (22a) that encourages the dancers. Girard destroys with a disciplined but furious competence while the crowd dances obliviously on, and Arnold gazes blankly, perhaps at the floor. All the while the music plays on, mechanically, acting as a double counterpoint to the periodic crashing of glass and to Arnold's quiet stillness amidst the flurry of movement. The music creates and underlines by its ironic, buoyant rhythm the absence of a fully unified emotional tone in the scene. Horror at the violence, yes, but a horror on the part of the spectator that is compromised by not being shared by anyone in the scene. When we look to Arnold, or to just anybody, for a reaction that would locate us within the scene, we are frustrated. The disjunction of music and action sets up an ironic counterpoint that denies the possibility of any simple identification or emotional analogy between spectator and the character. Arnold's situation—he is the good and helpless character—calls forth a feeling, but we are denied the grounds for identification, the perception of a relevant common trait, by his lack of response. We recognize in that kind of moment the difference between Arnold and ourselves. It is a difference which, to make sense of, we must locate in some other order of explanation than our current relation to the film. But the precise terms by which we could make sense of Arnold's action are not explicitly provided, and coming to terms with our uncertainty must be deferred or integrated with the film at its proper level. The result of the film's calling for and then denying our tendency to feelings of identification is a way of depicting character. It leaves us with the sense not that the character has no feeling, though the acting style precludes exteriorization in the sense of expressiveness, only that as spectators we have no immediately visible access to terms by which action might be comprehended.

That Arnold's passiveness is not to be mistaken for his being insensate or in a complete withdrawal from the world is amply demonstrated by his "dialogue" with his "friends" the road marker, the telephone pole and Balthazar (56–63). The effect of his soliloquy—it is the imagery that effects the sense of dialogue—is to temporarily reorder the relations between subjects and objects, specifically as Arnold relates to Balthazar. No man that lovingly animates the world of objects and feels with them the monotony of their being condemned to stay by the road "forever watching the same clods pass by" can be seen as an object. Yet his personification of these objects ("friends") introduces Arnold into the same order of being. Arnold declares the world alive. He locates Balthazar and himself in the world of objects and animates it.

The organization of the imagery confirms Arnold's mode of perception and places the spectator at such an angle to it that it enforces his assent to its legitimacy. Bresson does this by using the shot/reverse shot figure for the depiction of Arnold's mode of consciousness of the world without providing the spectator grounds for dissent. That we see Arnold looking and speaking to objects is less remarkable than the reverse shot of Arnold seen from an angle, as if it were the object returning, or acknowledging the capacity to return the look (58a, 61). That Bresson wishes us to understand this sequence as a depiction of the dialectical relation Arnold/world is made evident by the cuts (from 58b to 59 and from 61b to 62a) that articulate these reciprocal acts of perception. The return to almost the same profile (61b, 62a), but from a different camera position, underlines the importance of camera angle as such. Specifically, the angle down on Arnold (59, 61) as from the pole attests to the legitimacy of Arnold's investment in the consciousness and substantiality of the external world.

Arnold's lack of reaction to the cafe's destruction compromises the possibility of an explicitly moral condemnation of Girard from Arnold's, or the community's, point of view. The effect of the scene is to put into question the validity of our tendency for a moral response, and to turn the meaning of the scene both toward the irrational fact of the destruction shown by the images (33, 34, 35), and in a curious way, to the unreal or improbable quality of the community's non-response. The confrontation ends (36, 37, 38) by the repetition of the motif, the bang of the firecrackers and Balthazar's nervous jump, an explicitly formal device that we have seen already three times in the scene. It is a way the film comments on its own organization of images without being visually self-referential.

Constructing the text and locating the spectator within it through a denial of the possibility of identification with character proceeds by a coherent system of organization of filmic images. Images are only rarely referred to the glance or even interests of a character located in the story, and where they are, as in the regularly employed shot/reverse shot figure, the effect is to qualify, by a set of formal strategies, both our reading of the shot as characterizing the one doing the seeing, or encourage our identification with the one depicted. The four sub-units of the story (as defined by person and locale)—Balthazar, Marie and her mother, Arnold and Girard, Arnold and

Balthazar—are visually unrelated or discontinuous from each other. Marie's movement away (7, 8) and then back toward the cafe (42), linking her spatially with Girard, and the lawyer's exiting movement (50) are the only exceptions. The different locales inside and outside the cafe in which the action takes place are mediated by Balthazar's presence. Temporal continuity, the sense of succession and spatial integration of action in different places is achieved by three successive pieces of music that have a source, we discover (22a), within the space of the story. Changes in volume level designate the proximity of different actions to that source.

Within the instances of the shot/reverse shot, the film carefully delineates the difference between what the character is shown to see and what we see. The effect is to discriminate our location in space, where the camera is, from the matter of depicting the character's subjectivity. Arnold's and Girard's presence together during their encounter within the same frame (23–29), while conveying something of their dialectical relation, has the effect of distancing ourselves from either of their places. Where only one figure occupies the frame, as in shots of Marie and her mother, the effect of symmetrically reversing their places, especially when each figure is frontal and still, and when their eyes are down, is similar. The image is seen less as the image of the character as he/she experiences that situation. The framing is a triumph of formality different from the sense of the intensity of the written text of the dialogue. In its rigor and asceticism, and in its flattening of feeling, the framing corresponds more to the intonation of the performance of the text. It has the effect of a negation, and what it denies is the idea that difference of angle is capable of representing what a face or voice can not. The premises of the acting and of the découpage are coordinate: both put into effect a picture of a form of life, the understanding of whose interiority is altogether problematic, which is to say mysterious. This effort to preserve the mysteriousness of person is one side of the justification for a style that denies the possibility of an identification between character and spectator. It will take an analysis of the film's allegory to show how that psychological point is transformed into the religious image that Bresson proposes.

Linked in terms of its effect to the symmetry and frontality of the imagery is the radical shifting of set-up, 180 degrees, on the same character in successive shots. Thus the miser is shown (46, 47, 48) front to back to front. Similarly the mother (41, 42, 43) and Arnold. Such organization of imagery denies that there is or need be a field complementary to the one of the screen occupied by another witness or character who will appear in the countershot. Such a character can in fact appear, as with the exchanges between Girard and Arnold, but that does not imply that the image is the character's image or that he is necessary for its presentation. This use of inversion is an affirmation of volume. It undoes what Oudart calls the "system of the suture" and implies a critique of the premises by which a narrative system fictionally locates the spectator-in-the-text in the place of character. The sense of depicted space created by the film's succession of images from different set-ups is read less as the depiction or effect of the attention, consciousness, or judgment of character, than as recording the impersonality of the narrative syntax, which, however, the film does not expose or declare or point to as such. Rather, the spectator's feelings of the impersonality of the framing, occasioned by the dissociation of spatial location of the camera from inferences about the psychology of character, is an integral part of our own reading of Bresson's treatment of the problematics of disclosure of "character."

In this text, the forms of depiction generally do not designate or call attention to themselves. This sense of the integration of strategies of depiction with the spectator's response to character and the presentation of narrative (and the neutralization of self reference) is illustrated and confirmed by the way Bresson shows Girard breaking the mirror (in 30 and 33b, c). Such an illusion, of a reflected world in a frame, nearly indistinguishable from the frame of the image that encloses it, might be taken as an internal commentary, even allegory of some form of cinema. One might then note that Girard's absence from the film frame and virtual appearance in the mirror (the screen) in (30b) exemplifies the relation of camera (director) to character; that Girard's hand with bottle coming into and leaving the frame (30a, b) distinguishes our fictional position from his; and that the mirror, as opposed to the screen, is a surface that supports no illusory projections. The shot, however, lasts a very brief time. It is clearly related to the action of the story by what frames it (29b, 31a) and is discriminated from the space of the film by being shattered by something thrown from within that space. These facts encourage us to regard the moment in terms of the story, specifically Girard's relation to Arnold's scrutiny and his wish to avoid self-recognition. The film in other words locates the meaning of the event of breaking the mirror not at the level of a reflection on a mode of address to the spectator, as if the film were presenting itself as a reflexive object, but rather, at another level, as a sign of character.

The spectator's interest does not attach to the level of representation, that is, to the evidence or structure that relates to the question as to who is exhibiting these images, whether narrator or character. His interest is still in the characters and the story that unfolds in a depicted three-dimensional space. Yet, as between these two levels, referred to in Chapter 1 as the "ambiguity of the double origin" of the image, the spectator's position in the text is arbitrated by the narrator to both rivet his attention and debar him from identification. As such, the text redefines what is at issue in narrative continuity and the process and effects of reading. It amounts to this: that continuity in this text is defined not primarily by the maintenance of matches that guarantee the continuous succession and integration of action. Because of the formality of the representation, the image acquires a sense or a kind of presence, not fully located within or explained by the terms of the story. The interruption of our double tendency to identification with the formal "center" as a guarantor of spatial legibility, and with the emotional situation of character, constitutes an interruption and a redefinition of the "impression of the real" produced by reading. We see the film at the same time as both the story and as a succession of concrete images. The sense of continuity, assisted by music, is that of the imagery. Yet the film does not deprive these images of an actual and meaningful reference. In fact, the film asserts the importance of that reference hyperbolically through the extraordinary presence of "effects" on the sound track. The film defines its relation to the spectator as a mode of attention, a mode demanded by an adequate response to the elliptical features of these images, and not as a mode of transparency or identification. The "impression of reality" of the film is defined jointly as the reality of the discourse and the material reality to which it refers.

The general strategy of the film is a reconstruction of the process of fantasy, that in conventional rhetoric, establishes the relation between character and the (fictional) place of the spectator. By these means the film delimits the extent of the reader's participation. The film makes the spectator continually sensitive to the dissociation of narrator from character and of his literal position before the screen, not, so to speak, in-the-text. As such, there is a transformation of the way the point of view in the text is established and the way it orders meaning. The character Arnold, while defining a center of spectator interest, does not function unproblematically to mediate the view of the narrator to the spectator. In *Au Hasard, Balthazar*, the structure of surrogation, that in other texts governs the production and interpretation of meaning, is blocked and transformed by making Arnold, or Balthazar, an opaque center in a way that questions the meaning of what he sees. The result, for the principal features of the organization of meaning in the text, is a double or disjunct point of view in which the narrator's commentary is a product of a continuous but incomplete, and therefore distinct, effort to interpret and avoid misinterpreting this character. This interpretation is defined by the disjunct connection of the character with tonal features of the text, whether through the narrator's music or the beauty of nature. The narrator's view functions as an exegesis of the other's.

The allegorical structure and significance of the film is based on the meaning of Balthazar's life. This structure testifies to the divinity in or behind chance and human suffering by asking the audience's assent through its experience of that life. That life means what it does, though, only by reference to a human world, specifically to the life of Marie and her family, lover (Girard) and suitor (Jacques), and village inhabitants (baker, grain merchant, etc.). Balthazar acts as the thread which the film follows, situating Marie's fortunes against the background of her father's legal dispute and an obscure smuggling plot involving Arnold and Girard. Each episode is treated as the occasion for defining a linearity and a kind of eventfulness the film calls "chance," and for delineating a certain stage or condition of life.

The film does not restrict its representation of the making of Balthazar's life to the simple narrative recital of events. The text constitutes and puts into effect an interpretation of the story by means of two architectonic strategies: allegory and personification. For reasons appropriate to the ends he wishes to achieve, the narrator represents the story of this life by a figurative commentary. This design has an intricate textual logic. The allegory denies that the meaning(s) of Balthazar are defined by the character's actions toward and understanding of him, that his meaning exists exclusively on the literal level. The representation shows Balthazar as an opaque figure incomprehensible to human thought. By simultaneously exhibiting and blocking his literal meaning on the level of the story, and inhibiting our tendency to personification, the allegorical structure proposes a second, figurative level of meaning, that leads us to see Balthazar as a religious emblem whose life announces a Christian truth, the need for God's mercy.

The film continuously explores Balthazar's ambiguous existence as subject and/or object. He is connected to the lives of characters with a complex intimacy that affirms both. In the everyday world he shares with them, he is treated as an animal. As Bresson makes fully clear by a fastidious attention to the general economy of exchange, usually the passing of money and goods from one hand to another, Balthazar is a piece of property and a beast of burden. He can be used for the satisfaction of debts and bequeathed by wills; he pulls hay, draws a cart, delivers bread. At the same time, he is named and treated by people in ways that seem appropriate, and then only rarely, to human life: he is called a "genius" (circusman), a "saint" (Marie's mother), "son of the Devil" (Arnold). He is loved and abandoned by Marie; hated, burned, beaten by Girard; beaten and saved from the executioner's ax by Arnold. At the limit of this characterization is his part in Christian ritual. At the beginning of the film he is baptized and given the salt of wisdom. Toward the end, (after having been called a saint), he leads the funeral cortege of Marie's father, dressed in ecclesiastical vestments.

Balthazar is the center of successive emotional displacements and projections by others. How he is treated reflects less what he is than the way he is regarded. His very nature is to sustain; that is, neither to confirm or to deny, the validity of the way others regard him. With the exception of Marie who adores him and caresses and garlands his head, after an idyllic youth, he is treated cruelly by the world. He is almost always the object of another's action. Indissolubly joined with Marie's love is Girard's cruelty. Balthazar is beaten because he is a rival. At other times he is beaten for the same reason Girard pours oil on the road, simply because Girard is the way he is. Balthazar does not seem to welcome such beatings in any masochistic sense. He is beaten as a rival because Girard attributes to him a reciprocal love for Marie. But being the object for her passion is not something within his power either to cause, to stop, or to take responsibility for. Does Girard imagine that these beatings would cause the animal to cease his affection for another? In this love triangle—Marie's passion, Girard's jealousy and anger, Balthazar's innocence—Balthazar suffers in a way that the film shows we are not in a position to understand. We do not know what makes sense to him. We see only that he is beaten. His jumping at the sound of exploding firecrackers and other responses make it clear he is not insensible.

However opaque Balthazar is, the motivation for action on him is typically represented in terms of economics or a psychology of love and masochism. That is, Balthazar takes different roles according to the interests of his masters. Often his masters are characterized in the fashion of medieval allegory as sins—Pride, Avarice, Gluttony, etc. Characters act in a way that film invites us to consider as realistic, according to feelings of power, love, shame, desire, avarice, pride, will, etc. People act or avoid acting, the film suggests, because of such "reasons."

Balthazar does not have the same meaning in the film as he does for the characters. The difference is structured by, and is the structure of, the allegory. On the level of the story, the meaning of Balthazar's status as subject or object, the role of circumstance and accident, and suffering, is stated and resolved by the action of characters toward each other and toward him. We understand this behavior in psychological terms. On the level of the representation, our understanding of Balthazar in the chain of events that constitute the plot (designated by the title as "chance") takes on a different, specifically more ecstatic, more profound, religious significance.

The first function of the allegory is the blocking, perhaps we might say the veiling, of a certain more apparent reading. Structures of contradiction, enigma, and incompleteness work in carefully designed ways to frustrate a fully comprehensible following of the film. We do not know, for example, exactly what the relation is between Arnold, Girard, the murder, the police, and the smuggling. Or we are confronted by plain contradiction: Jacques's father says in one shot that he will not have Balthazar, and we see him in the next taking him away; or an action leads to an unexpected result, as in Arnold's being rewarded by an inheritance immediately after trying to kill the Captain of Police. Explanations, like so many facts, causes, or results, are withheld. The effect is a sense of witnessing events, which because they have (apparently) significant but mysterious causes elsewhere, cannot be fully understood. It is a strategy that makes the events we do see, like the open combat between Arnold and Girard, or like Arnold's death, full of a meaning that we are uncertain about how to locate, and whose decipherment implies and requires a background that is permanently out of reach.

Withholding, veiling, and masking work at several levels of the text: in the organization of facts in the story, the depiction of action in planes of the single image, and in the relation between the narrator's conception of character and the vision the spectator has of him. Stylistically, these structures of contradiction, veiling, and partial disclosure block a certain form of determinate resolution, frustrate our understanding, and make a simple reading of the action obviously inadequate. The scene under consideration, for instance, implies an understanding between Arnold and his antagonists that the spectator does not quite know how to define. Arnold's destiny foreseen and planned by Girard, and agreed to by Arnold, takes the form of a mutually acknowledged ritual: their putting him on Balthazar, the kisses, the ironic salutation "brother," the goodbyes. The sequence of these events, unexpected insofar as they are determined by an unknown ritual, refers to an order of behavior, a compact whose terms are only implicit. The ritual gives the unfolding events a meaning that refers to some inexplicit order, specifically not that of the plot, which in accord with its complex ellipses, has a gap on the precise point necessary for us to understand this killing as justified revenge for some specific betrayal. Rather, the significance of Arnold's death, and Girard's role in it, is articulated in terms of an implicit analogy. Through a distant parallelism, the film evokes a contrast between these images and events—the road, the donkey saved from death by the man of peace who rides him, the doctrine of friendship—and those of the New Testament. Never does the film imply any precise analogy between Balthazar or Arnold or Christ. Their lives are too different. But the film does show quite explicitly that Balthazar passes through life periods designated as spiritual stages. Bresson, it is clear, is not speaking simply of animals, but by analogy, of the humble of spirit. As such, Balthazar is the explicit vehicle of personification of the Christian soul. When the events of the story of Balthazar's life come to be seen as the text that supports an allegorical interpretation, whether or not that story bears an exact analogy, as stations on the road, to some other more perfect life, the meaning of events like Arnold's death are transformed. For whatever reason—contradiction, gap, enigma—the inexplicability is a condition of the coming, or perhaps the announcement of a second, superordinate significance.

The mediating structures effect a transit of meaning from a literal to a figurative level. The various strategies of "veiling"—ellipsis, reversal of cause and effect, etc.—demonstrate the inadequacy of a literal reading and invite another. The segmentation of the body by the frame, particularly the isolation of hands and feet, promotes an attention to the instrumentalities of action. As a stylistic feature, framing is thus integrated with the picture of psychological determinations, the will, that the film seeks to read at another level through the interventions of chance. In general, the complex of images—sheep, donkey, water, road—while located firmly and "realistically" in the locale, provide the potential grounds for a religious significance.

The music in the film, in its organization of significant oppositions, functions to the same end: to establish a thematic contrast that creates and orders the text's figurative sense. Jazz or rock, as played on Girard's transistor, or on the jukebox, define the musical world of the "story," and locates that world in a particular historical time—with cars and motorbikes. The Schubert Sonata Number 20, which is expressly designated as the narrator's musical "voice" by its appearance over the titles, has the connotations of a past age, and stands essentially in opposition to the modernity of the story. It stops, though, to make room for, and to set off, Balthazar's braying. The prominent opposition, motorbike/Balthazar, establishes an historical affinity between Balthazar and the Schubert, as both being old-fashioned, of another age. The Schubert's appearance in the body of the film itself, from its first introduction, is shown to have a close relation to the sweetest period of Balthazar's life, his childhood. As Balthazar-child looks on, Jacques and Marie sit on the swing beneath a huge tree, in the bliss of childhood romance. The Schubert is associated too, with the memory of that moment, for when years later, Balthazar returns (twice) to the farm and strolls past the bench beneath the tree, the same music reminds us of the ecstatic, lost time. In general though, the music stands in marked contrast to Balthazar's current, adult suffering. It accompanies moments of anguish, pain, and death. Through its reference to the past, its association with present suffering sets up structures of emotional dislocation and contradiction that encourages us to see another, intensified, meaning in the events of the story. Eroticism, cruelty and death, when juxtaposed with the music, take on a more mysterious and sublime sense. Like the other mediating structures, the music works by disjuncture, not analogy, to bring into effect a second sense that contests and sometimes transforms the first.

Even when this (potential) structure of interpretation is in effect, the significance of characters' actions are depicted as being psychologically, not allegorically, determined. Establishing the integrity of the literal level of the film is a major concern of the text. This feature of the film is evident, for example, in this sequence, in the relation between Marie and her mother. The delivery of lines, the direction of their glances, looking up when they speak and then down, describes a psychological dynamic of headstrong rebellion and the assertion of parental authority.

The manner of characterization in general is linked in a complex way to the differentiation between the two levels of meaning in the text, the literal and the figurative. The film asks us to consider the depiction of character in terms of a difference, though not a separation, between surface and depth, outside and inside. While it does not deny a profound sensibility, the manner of acting affirms as noncontradictory both that the body is a picture of the soul, and also that the exteriorization or disclosure of that being-in-flesh is less (spiritually) than there is. Bresson's direction of actors is a rejection of the view that a necessary and unambiguous relationship exists between outside and inside. The result makes the precise nature of the depicted interiority systematically ambiguous.

This ambiguity is the premise that determines our perception of character as subject or object. Because of the way he suffers the action of others with such extraordinary restraint, the Bressonian character, like Balthazar, might be mistakenly thought to be insensible, beyond or without feeling. But the film shows this conclusion is emphatically not the case. The sensibility of a character or of Balthazar, in one of its aspects, is established by the heightened presence of certain sounds. When we take these sounds as representations of sensations, they imply, by analogy, a heightened but unexpressed form of interiority. Thus the picture of Balthazar's pain, the materiality of his body, and his confinement (slavery), are made fully explicit to the spectator-auditor through the sound of his feet on the pavement, his braying, the constant rattle of his chains, the closing of the gate of his stall, and the dull thuds of the beatings.

Such concrete descriptions of the sensations of character, even though the film demonstrates that inferences about subjectivity are problematic, establishes a fully credible animate world, remote from abstract terms of allegorical system. The depiction in psychological terms of the story of Marie, her family and Girard—their cruelty, love, eroticism, pride, and suffering—conforms to the cannons of strict realism.

The impression of reality of the story is strengthened by locating that action in real settings, whose full materiality and affect on the characters, is evident. Thus the important role of the representation of Nature and locale in the film. The village, the abandoned house, the fields of the farm, the place where Girard and Marie make love, Arnold's shack, the road, natural waterfalls, are all shown as parts of a verdant Nature, stirred by the wind, full of blossoming spring, and brilliantly and sensually lit up in a palette of tones that often reflects the subdued, glowing light of the late afternoon. Long shots, particularly of the roads and fields with the snowcapped mountains (from which Balthazar descended) in the furthest background, depict the character's place in the larger order of things. Critical scenes, of Marie's seduction or the conversations with Jacques on the bench, that mark her fall, are both primarily depicted in medium close-up shots. Nature is amply present in both, either as a vista, the sound of birds, or as the movement of wind and trees. In dramatic scenes, Nature is in the background, not fully in focus, but represented impressionistically by a glow and shadow from the reflected light on the trees and by the chirping of birds. Outdoor action unfolds in the full scenic volume of Nature. The organization of the action within the image validates the literality of the story by creating an impression of life grounded in the characters' existence in a real world. This "realism" is the film's response to the problem of authenticating its claims. The image of Balthazar's life demands that the depicted world locate characters, coincidence, Nature, and Balthazar himself. This the film accomplishes by locating the allegorical meaning in the world.

The film declares its interpretation of the depicted world by the ambiguous image of Balthazar's eye. On the level of the story only twice is an image associated with his glance. The sequence of shot/reverse shots in the garden with Marie suggests that Balthazar returns Marie's look. The most striking instance, though, is the moment in the circus, when again by a series of shot/reverse shots, Balthazar exchanges glances with a tiger, monkey, and elephant. This memorable sequence makes several points: that Balthazar can look and be looked at; that he does in fact have a view; and that the form of consciousness that belongs to Balthazar manifests itself in terms irreducible to the apprehension by a human consciousness. This exchange implies a being not restricted to experiencing bodily sensation, as for example, pain. But neither does it define, indeed it explicitly refuses to suppose it could define, the nature of that irreducible interiority. Balthazar's status as an intelligent being or as a witness, is linked both to his glance and to an incapacity to speak a language that humans can understand. His braying, which is given particular significance by interrupting the music (Schubert sonata) of the credits, which then resumes, has the effect of an absolutely expressive language whose motivation or meaning is as unintelligible as his glance. The contrast signifies that Balthazar has a voice whose inarticulateness and distance from music is nevertheless a form of feeling in that animal body.

Balthazar's eye as a sign of his being has a place of importance in the film that transcends any definition he is given by the story. He is transformed by the allegory from object to a mysterious, religious subject. The parallel to human spiritual trials does not specify his significance but creates an experience that points toward it. The allegory gives Balthazar a prominence, on the level of the film, as a witness, presence, or judge, that he lacks in the depicted world. His place on the level of the representation, as an eye, corresponds to an independent spatial mode. The space he occupies is often, especially in close-up, distinguished from that of the action. He is, for example, in the sequence under discussion, inserted in the space at formal junctures, in a way that breaks up and closes a train of human action. In another scene, Marie uses Balthazar as a barrier to (seem to) prevent Girard from catching her. The camera repeatedly shows close-ups of Balthazar blinking impassively in the center of a flurry of action, and seeming by his passivity to refuse to intervene to save Marie.

This refusal of a response is the primary strategy for delimiting the spectator's tendency to personify, or to identify with Balthazar, of denying that he is someone capable of sustaining our wishes. Balthazar is not regarded as he is on the level of the story. The narrator's representation returns Balthazar to his objecthood, but reinstates on the level of the film, his ambiguous status as subject. The allegory puts into effect, by structures of "veiling" and characterization, an interpretation that transforms Balthazar's ambiguity, as subject and object, into a sign of annunciation of the truth. It translates the literal meaning of events into a new and superordinate, a religious, system. It simultaneously affirms their literality and shows us that the allegorical meaning of such events, governed by chance, are believable because they were, from the start, immanent in the literal.

Balthazar's eye, hyperbolically stated by Bresson on the level of the film, transforms the donkey to the mysterious subjectivity of one blessed by grace, the saint. Focused on us, as much as anyone else, the eye does not embarrass us, but remains enigmatic. Though transformed into a subject, Balthazar is not personified. The incommensurability between us remains. That the final effect of the film is an experience of love makes our appreciation of the allegory, nevertheless, an aesthetic one.

The film *Au Hasard, Balthazar* explicitly locates the "story" as an object in the imaginative space that the narrator and spectator share. The narrator, having conceived of Balthazar as the central figure, makes his own position in the text problematical. It is problematical at the level of the motivation, functioning, and design of the entire text: in the relation between the work and its spectator. The issue which requires defining the relationship between the film and the "story" is not solved, though, simply by the text's calling attention to the procedures of composition or dramatizing the narrator's productive agency, by being explicitly self-reflexive. Where the spectator's belief in this religious view is made the basis of the text's claim to truth, what is at issue is an accounting, in terms of the call for authentication, of the standing of the one who shows us this world. The film employs a rhetoric that addresses the question of the standing of the narrator in relation to the story in two ways.

It explicitly depicts the story as an object ordered by chance. That is, it shows the succession of events that constitute the story as guided, apparently, by a logic and rationale other than that of one that controls the discourse. It exposes the events as lacking, indeed flaunting, an artistic necessity. The film depicts the separation of cause and effect, the miscarrying of intention, and the intervention of an order that makes will ineffectual. The opposition that we sense between the disorderliness of the story and the synthetic organization of an allegorical meaning, draws attention to the significance of chance as a means of ordering in its own right. The title, *Au*

Hasard, Balthazar, announces and confirms this theme, if read as Bresson's answer to an implied question (put by someone speaking for Balthazar) about why the world is as it is. The point is that the spectator sees the organization of events as an object that exists in its own right, as following an order of determination that stands independent either of characters' wishes, or of the narrator's intent. The film, however, does not *explicitly* refer to itself, or offer reflection on itself, in order to affirm this independence. The extraordinary formality of the level of representation—its elaborate ensemble of parallels, antitheses, comparisons, and reversals, serving to establish and make meaning of Balthazar's relations to the human world—sets off the story as such. Exhibition of the world of story, I have pointed out, is not correlated with any noticeable flattening of the image, nor with recording any obvious traces of the work of composition. The rationale for setting the text off as an object with this kind of formality has to do, I think, with realizing certain communicative ends, of establishing the conditions of a believable, religious world, and determining our relation to it as an aesthetic image.

Second, the film, in its fashion, explicitly locates the narrator. The narrator represents himself in the text, allegorically, as the eye of Balthazar. No attention is explicitly, or reflexively, drawn to this identification. But Balthazar's formal position in the text, as an eye (his insertion, in the sequence for example, at formal points of opening and closure) and the interpretation that it makes, corresponds to the point of view on and in the film. It is a nonmoralizing, lucid view of the facts of existence as seen by the camera. In this sense the narrator-eye is not just behind the camera but represents the function of the camera in the depicted world. As an eye, Balthazar is a subject, distinct from the space of the story, existing only on the level of the representation. Seeing his eye and presence in the text transforms, allegorically, the meaning of the story. In his identification with Balthazar, the narrator literally represents himself as existing at the level of the film, as the one whose view makes the meaning of the story. He allegorizes himself as the maker of the interpretation and locates himself in the only position he could occupy in a text, as *in*-the-text, in the space of intersubjective signification.

But the camera, however lucid its regard, has access to subjectivity only through what it can show. Appearance though, the film discloses, like the face of a character, is as much a veiling as a disclosure. The allegory takes on the function of revealing behind appearances a hidden truth of interiority. The text turns this skepticism in the form of the disjuncture inside/outside, into a demonstration of a religious form of life. The spectacle is meant not to be penetrated, nor can it, but to be seen as an image. By regarding Balthazar theologically, the text makes the narrator's reading of the story, strictly speaking, an exegesis.

The rhetoric of the film situates our relation to the character and to his story so as to appreciate its meaning. Within the requirements of authentication, it exhibits the film as an aesthetic image. By explicitly dissociating our view from that of the characters, through the construction of a double point of view, the narrator transforms our reading of the story: we attend equally to it and to the form of its presentation. The situation of the character provokes feelings of sympathy and pity. This Bresson can count on. But the distancing presence of the representation, as such, restrains our tendency toward attachment to, that is identification with, the character. "Character" is defined by the text as a screen or barrier as much as a medium of depiction. The result is that the text negates the efficacy of the rhetoric that in other styles gives the spectator a sense of access to character's interiority. The rhetoric of "transparency" is displaced, but only in the sense that in this text it serves fundamentally different ends: it establishes a religious depth and a redefinition of the significance of the "real."

So far as it is organized around the lucid but impassive eye of Balthazar, the film as a whole withholds grounds for the spectator's moral identification. Its point of view is explicitly not a moral one. The injustice is too great. Good and bad are facts, as if seen from a great height. The Bressonian rhetoric serves the ends of authentication by restraining our identification with character and showing the depicted world as an object of contemplation. Even though he is allegorized as the Christian soul, in the text he does not sustain our human projections. He can not stand as our double or as our brother. The result is that our "reading" of the "character" is defined not as a mirroring, imitation, or reflection, but as our experience of an otherness to be apprehended only by a figurative representation. Having felt the power, mystery and beauty of the image of that life, we are asked to acknowledge the claims of faith. We are pressed to consider the possibilities of interpretation. It is a rhetoric that delineates the limits of knowledge and of reading.

The narrator, in authenticating a religiously defined "impression of the real" by giving a picture of the depth of the story, undertakes to make clear the nature of his own powers and of his relation to the spectator. The film as a whole suggests that reflection on his constitutive powers, and on his authority to speak in an authentically religious mode, brings him to acknowledge, as he confronts the meaning of the Other, the limits of his textual function. The film's form is based on disjunct views. The "narrator's point of view," then, is a product of a distinct effort to avoid misrepresenting the knowledge he has of this special character and to record the effect of this reserve in the style. The spectator, faced by this declaration and by a filmic rhetoric designed to dissociate shots from inferences about characters' views and from narrative point of view, is in a reflective position to appreciate what he is to do. As a scene of instruction, the film demonstrates that the art of viewing, and in particular the role of emotional projection in "reading," needs to be reformulated. That we do not, finally, recognize Balthazar as what we think we are, should not, the film implies, stop us from loving him just the same.

Appendix C

Stills and Dialogue from
Au Hasard, Balthazar

Fade in.
Popular music with source in "story".
Song I (1–21)
Bang. Bang.

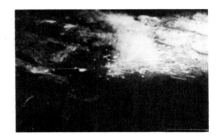

1

(off) Bang.
GIRARD. (off) Come in. Arnold's buying
the drinks.

2

GIRARD. Come on. Drinks on Arnold.

3

4a

MISER. (b) Is it true about the legacy?
LAWYER. Yes, his uncle has died and left him everything.

4b

5a

LAWYER. No doubt about the validity. Just a few formalities. (b)

5b

6

7

MARIE. I knew you'd come.
MOTHER. Is it wrong of me?

8

MARIE. You're always spying on me.

9

MOTHER. I wanted to know what you are
doing.

10

(off) Bang.

11

12

13

Bang.

14

(off) Bang.
Rattle of chains.

15

MOTHER. What do you see in this young
man?
MARIE. (off) I love him.

16

MARIE. You can't explain love.
If he tells me to do a thing. . .

17

MARIE. (off) . . .I do it.
MOTHER. Poor child.

18

MARIE. I'd follow him to the ends of the earth. If he asked me to . . .

19

MARIE. (off) . . .I'd kill myself for him. (off) Bang.

20

(off) Bang. Bang.
Song I stops.

21

Song II starts (22–43)

22a

22b

23a

(b) GIRARD. Not breaking anything? You're not angry?

23b

24

25a

(b) GIRARD. Drink you idiot.

25b

26

GIRARD. You worthless trash.

27

28

29a

29b

30a

30b

(c) Crash.

30c

31a

31b

(c) Crash.

31c

(off) Crash. Crash.

32

Crash.

33a

33b

33c

Crash.

34

Crash.

35

36

Bang.

37

(off) Bang.
Rattle of chains.

38

MOTHER. Your father is suffering. He
lives. . .

39

MOTHER. (off) . . .only to love us.
MARIE. He loves his sorrow more than us.
He cultivates it. He needs it.

40

MOTHER. It's the last thing I beg you.

41

MOTHER. Come home with me. Otherwise we'll bring you by force.

42

Marie's footsteps.
Song II ends.
Song III begins (43–49)

43

MARIE. (a) Save me. Take me away.

44a

44b

45

MISER. Your father will tear you apart.

46

MARIE. Papa is obsessed with me.
YOUNG MAN. If you want her pay!

47

48

Dissolve.
Song III dissolves into sound of sweeping
of broken glass.

49a

49b

50

Rattle of chain.

51

52

GIRARD. Good old Arnold.

53

GIRARD. -(a) Going a long way Arnold?
Are you leaving us?
ARNOLD. Yes.
GROUP. Long live Arnold!

54a

GIRARD. Long live Arnold!
Thud of a kick. (b)

54b

Balthazar's hooves on pavement.

55

Fade out. Fade in.

56a

56b

ARNOLD. (c) Goodbye. . .

56c

ARNOLD. (off) . . .my old and trusted friend condemned to stay here forever. . .

57

ARNOLD. (a) . . .seeing the same clods pass by.

58a

58b

ARNOLD. Goodbye, old pal.

59

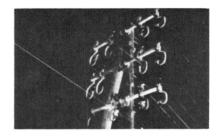

60

Distant horn.

61a

61b

ARNOLD. (a) And what about you, old friend?

62a

62b

Thud of head hitting pavement.

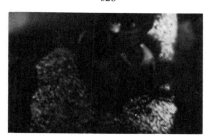

63a

63b

Postscript

Analysis of the relation between narrative incident and imagery in the film-text requires distinguishing among its several levels of organization and determination. The body of this study provides the terms to account for the significant structural mediations within the text between the functions of narrator, character, and spectator. Together these analyses of specific films and the attending concepts, distinctions, and procedures embedded in those analyses, constitute a description of a rhetorical level of organization of narrative film-texts. In this context narration can be described as the act, realized through formal structures of mediation (like center, shift, prohibition, surrogation, continuity) of telling a story, and of determining and locating these three functions—narrator, character, spectator—in fictional "places" in the discourse.

What these structures mediate is the relation between a technical level ("shots" and "set-ups") and the fictional level that designates views and point of view. The study of the films shows the necessity and productiveness of distinguishing these levels of description and of analyzing in detail the structural means by which they are coordinated and made significant in different texts. Representation of a character's "view" seldom corresponds to a coincidence of his glance with the camera, though it does with the Crofter and with Lucy. In the case of Hannay, though, while facing him, the camera depicts the field of his visual search and represents his estimation of the situation. Likewise, the sequence from *Stagecoach* depicts Dallas's view even though it makes the point that in the story, she believes she has no significant view. Both Arnold and Balthazar are shown looking, but the tendency within the text to dissociate shots from views, makes comprehension of these "views" problematic. This form of depiction makes viewing itself the subject of interest and suggests how a "conventional" text puts into play a rhetorical system that converts the presentation of shots into a reading of views. The evaluation of characters' views by the assertion of the narrator's point of view works on another level. The system which allows the making of such inferences between levels of shot, view, and point of view is the mechanism of the narration.

The difference between the rhetorical organization of *Stagecoach* and *The 39 Steps*, taken together, and *Au Hasard, Balthazar*, might clarify and summarize the terms of the basic structure of mediation: the narrator's interpretation of the meaning of the story by point of view, and the reader's place in its apprehension. The paradigms that define these contrasting rhetorics—"transparent" (*Stagecoach, The 39 Steps*) and "opaque" (*Au Hasard, Balthazar*)—arbitrate the relations between the two levels in the text, representation and story, by different systems of interpretation. The rhetoric of "transparency" is based on a confidence that the narrator can locate and determine the significance of each feature in the film in terms of a coherence ordered about the fictional relation (of surrogation) between narrator and character. The reading of diverse features of the text—lighting, rhythm, set-ups, etc.—is performed in accord, as by analogy, with a description, report, or presentation of the interests of the central character. The spectator sees and is involved in the story by a form of emotional participation and identification with this figure. This commitment, distinct from the structure through which the spectator's formal location is established, is the "point" around which the structure of values or judgments, whatever form it takes, is constituted. In the case at hand, *Stagecoach*, point of view delineates the social norm of right and wrong through Dallas and Lucy and condemns the system that enforces such prejudice. In *The 39 Steps* the danger to Hannay posed by the Crofter's misperception sustains our appreciation of the ambiguity of Hannay's situation. In these instances, the interests of the central character and those of the narrator converge in a way that effaces the narrator's report of the action. The system of "interpretation" that negotiates the relation of levels in the text suppresses the impersonal, formal mechanisms of the narration and the means by which the spectator is engaged in the view of the character. The narrator defines the meaning of the shots as views by the construction of "character." The significance of action and character are transparent to the spectator in the sense that the structures that mediate representation and story, and text and culture, are readily negotiated by a kind of recognition of psychological or social types, existing outside the text, without an apparent interpretation.

The relation between the levels of representation and story in the paradigm of "opaqueness" (*Au Hasard, Balthazar* is an example) is mediated by an explicit system of exegesis. The text in its internal organization is explicitly connected with the problem of the relation between the character's appearance and interiority, and the narrator's means of depiction. The point of view in the work, established in *Au Hasard, Balthazar* through a dissociation of locale or music from the sense of the action, is overtly a product of disjunction between the views of character and the authority of the narrator. The foregrounding of the narrative structure exposes the role of chance, and disengages the motivation of character from the sequence of the action. By questioning the pattern of inference that associates shots with views, the rhetoric makes viewing itself, the character's view of the world, and the spectator's view of the film as an object, a subject of interest and reflection. Between the two levels of discourse, the text establishes a system of interpretive protocols and procedures that block conventional "transparent" readings, and puts into effect, by certain codes specific to the text, an allegorical meaning. In this sense the opaque text simply makes explicit the way meaning is produced in any text. The effort at authentication—of locating the narrator-in-the-text and the spectator before it—and prescribing the terms of the text's validity by ways restricted to those within its own command, is a sign of the narrator's explicit attempt to locate the text within the culture at large. That is to say, the point of view of the text advances an interpretation of the story, proposes a reflection on its own constituitive powers, and situates itself in a cultural history.

In the way it presents the world through a character, the rhetoric functions as a medium of communication with the spectator. By insuring the impression of a continuous reality, the formal mechanisms of the narrative, particularly centering and continuity, constitute and maintain a continuous fictional identity for the viewing subject: his role as site of the action, the *locus dramaticus*. Further, the rhetoric locates the spectator in a fictional order other than the one where he sees himself to be, namely in an imaginative order of projection, recognition, and "force"—the realm of fictional figures and of identifications. The relation between the formal means of presentation described on the literal levels as shots (scale, angle, etc.) and the narratological level (by centering), is distinct, obviously not from the delineation of "views," but from the realm of identifications and the narrator's judgments. The meaningful reality of the discourse, the depicted world, depends primarily on its capacity to evoke belief, on the force of the spectator's identification with or interest in character. In a Freudian sense the realm of identifications constitutes what might be called the scene of instruction. In this connection, what the two abstract paradigms describe are the limiting terms of the spectator's apprehension of the human-object: as his double and as the irreducible "other." A structure of identification, in which the character acts as the medium of depiction, guarantees the transmission of cultural forms, and gives access to and orders a recognizable world. A structure of attention, by explicitly locating the spectator outside the character, raises the possibility of the appearance of another form of self-perspective. What we have learned from film as a scene of instruction might validly be called a form of its cultural history.

Bibliography

Auerback, Erich. "Odysseus' Scar," chap. 1, *Mimesis*. Princeton: Princeton University Press, 1953.

Barthes, Roland. "An Introduction to the Structural Analysis of Narrative." *New Literary History*, vol. 6, no. 3, Winter 1975.

Baudry, Jean Louis. "Ideological Effects of the Basic Cinematographic Apparatus." *Film Quarterly*, vol. 28, no. 2, Winter 1974–75.

Baxtin, Mixail. "Discourse Typology in Prose," *Readings in Russian Poetics*, Ladislav Matejka and Krystyna Pomorska, eds. Cambridge, Mass: The M.I.T. Press, 1971.

Bazin, André. *"Le Journal d'un Curé de Campagne* and the Stylistics of Robert Bresson," *What is Cinema?*, vol. 1. Hugh Gray tr. Berkeley: University of California Press, 1967.

Bloomfield, Morton. "Authenticating Realism and the Realism of Chaucer." *Thought*, no. 39, 1964.

Bresson, Robert. "Entretien: Robert Bresson par Jean Luc Godard et Michel Delahaye. *Cahiers du Cinéma*, No. 178, Mai 1966.

Cahiers du Cinéma. "Balthazar au hasard—Table ronde." *Cahiers du Cinéma*, no. 180.

Cavell, Stanley. *The World Viewed*. New York: The Viking Press, 1971.

Comolli, Jean Louis. "Technique et Idéologie: Caméra, perspective profondeur de champ." *Cahiers du Cinéma*, no. 229, May-June 1971.

Dayan, Daniel. "The Tutor Code of Classical Cinema: A Semiological Study of J. P. Oudart's Theory of Signification." Master's thesis, Stanford University, 1973.

————. "The Tutor Code of Classical Cinema." *Film Quarterly*, vol. 28, no. 1, Fall 1974.

Derrida, Jacques. "Structure, Sign and Play in the Discourse of the Human Sciences," *The Structuralist Controversy*, Richard Macksey and Eugenio Donato, eds. Baltimore: The Johns Hopkins Press, 1970.

Fish, Stanley. "Literature in the Reader: Affective Stylistics." *New Literary History*, vol. 2, no. 1, Autumn 1970.

Foucault, Michel. "Las Meninas," chap. 1, *The Order of Things*. New York: Pantheon Books, 1970.

Freud, Sigmund. "Instincts and Their Vicissitudes," *Standard Edition*, vol. 14. London: Hogarth Press.

————. "Identification," *Standard Edition*, vol. 18. London: Hogarth Press.

Fried, Michael. "Toward a Supreme Fiction: Genre and Beholder in the Art Criticism of Diderot and His Contemporaries." *New Literary History*, vol. 6, no. 3, Spring 1975.

Guzzetti, Alfred. "The Role of Theory in Films and Novels." *New Literary History*, vol. 3, no. 1, 1971–72.

————. "Narrative and the Filmic Image." *New Literary History*, vol. 6, no. 2, Winter 1975.

Heath, Stephen. "Lessons from Brecht." *Screen*, vol. 15, no. 2, Summer 1974.

Iser, Wolfgang. "Interdeterminacy and the Reader's Response," *Aspects of Narrative*, J. Hillis Miller, ed. New York: Columbia University Press, 1971.

―――. *The Implied Reader*. Baltimore: The Johns Hopkins University Press, 1974.

Jauss, Hans Robert. "Levels of Identification of Hero and Audience." *New Literary History*, vol. 5, no. 2, Winter 1974.

Kermode, Frank. "Novels: Recognition and Deception." *Critical Inquiry*, vol. 1, no. 1, September 1974.

Kristeva, Julia. *Semeiotike: Recherches pour une Sémanalyse*. Paris. Editions du Seuil, 1969.

―――. "The Ruins of a Poetics," *Russian Formalism*, Stephen Barr and John Bowlt, eds. Edinburgh: Scottish Academic Press, 1973.

Laffey, Albert. "Le Récit, Le Monde et le Cinéma," chap. 3, *Logique du Cinema*. Paris: Masson et Cie, 1964.

Lubbock, Percy. *The Craft of Fiction*. New York: The Viking Press, 1957.

Metz, Christian. *Langage et cinéma*. Paris: Librairie Larousse, 1971.

Mitry, Jean. *Esthétique et Psychologie du Cinéma*. vol. 1: section 2, "L'Image filmique." Vol. 2: Section 4, "Rythme et prises de vues mobiles." Paris: Editions Universitaires, 1965.

Nietzsche, Friedrich. *The Birth of Tragedy*, Walter Kauffman, tr. New York: Vintage Books, 1967.

Oudart, Jean-Pierre. "La Suture." *Cahiers du Cinéma*, No. 211.

―――. "La Suture." *Cahiers du Cinéma*, No. 212.

―――. "L'effect de reel." *Cahiers du Cinéma*, No. 228.

Poulet, Georges. "Criticism and the Experience of Interiority," *The Structuralist Controversy*, Richard Macksey and Eugenio Donato, eds. Baltimore. The Johns Hopkins Press, 1970.

Prokosh, Michael. "Bresson's Stylistics." *Film Quarterly*, vol. 25, no. 2, 1971–72.

Ricour, Paul. "Metaphor and the Main Problem of Hermeneutics." *New Literary History*, vol. 6, no. 1.

Ropars-Wuilleumier, Marie-Claire. "Un Mauvais Reve." *Esprit*, June 1966.

―――. "Narration et Signification: un exemple filmique." *Poétique*, no. 12, 1972.

Todorov, Tzvetan. "Les categories du recit littéraire." *Communications*, no. 8, 1966.

―――. *Littérature et Signification*. Paris: Librairie Larousse, 1967.

―――. "Problems de L'enonciation." *Langages*, no. 17, March 1970.

―――. "On Linguistic Symbolism." *New Literary History*, vol. 6, no. 1, Autumn 1974.

―――. "La lecture comme construction." *Poétique*, no. 24, 1975.

Warshow, Robert. "*Day of Wrath*: The Enclosed Image," *Film Theory and Criticism*, Gerald Mast and Marshall Cohen, eds. New York: Oxford University Press, 1974.